Gift of the Soul

A Spiritual Journey

Dale Colclasure
David Jensen

May your life's journey
be filled with never ending
wonder & adventure!
Dale Colclasure

Rainbow Pride Press, LLC
Boulder, Colorado USA

www.RainbowPridePress.com

Published by:

Rainbow Pride Press, LLC
6525 Gunpark Drive, Suite #150-117
Boulder, Colorado USA 80301
(303) 267-2155
(303) 543-0026 Fax
Email: EditorRPP@aol.com
www.RainbowPridePress.com

Publisher's Cataloging-in-Publication Data

Colclasure, Dale.
Gift of the soul : a spiritual journey / by Dale Colclasure, David Jensen. -- 1st ed.
p. cm.
LCCN 2002090543
ISBN 0-9703988-1-6

1. Spiritual life--Fiction. 2. Gays--Fiction.
I. Jensen, David, 1963- II. Title.

PS3603.O5344G54 2002 813'.6
QBI33-221

Cover designed by Tabitha Manresa
Cover art used by permission — Steve Walker

Who in the world am I? Ah, that's the great puzzle.

—Lewis Carroll

Dedication

To our families and friends who gave us the strength and encouragement to undertake this project and fulfill a lifelong dream. To all those who have impacted and influenced our lives, making us the individuals we are today, "Thank You!" The spiritual journey we both pursue has been enriched because of your unconditional love and light.

—Dale Colclasure
—David Jensen

Introduction

It has been said, "Coincidences are miracles in which God wishes to remain anonymous."

During the course of time that it took to write this book, we experienced a number of these miracles.

One day, while walking a familiar sidewalk in Boulder, Dale noticed a lone envelope lying face down on the sidewalk; something inside him said, *"Pick it up."*

He picked it up. The envelope had no return address, but was addressed to a nonprofit organization in Boulder County.

Dale delivered it to the nonprofit agency that very day. The office manager opened the unmailed envelope, which contained an anonymous check in the amount of $500. The office manager was overwhelmed with joy. She thanked Dale profusely for hand-delivering the check, which may have never made it to its final destination. A previously written portion of **GIFT OF THE SOUL** features a similar act of unconditional love.

During Christmas, David received a small key chain with an LED light on the end. The light, when illuminated, casts the clearest and sharpest indigo color one could imagine. Indigo is the color that we imagined coming from the cave in **GIFT OF THE SOUL**.

On more than one occasion, we both encountered the beauty of a single red rose. The red rose appears throughout **GIFT OF THE SOUL** and represents the truest symbol of unconditional love. Although a red rose is by no means a hard-to-find item, the places we encountered them were.

Another day, Dale was walking past a church, which recently had had its western facing doors remodeled and repaired—doors that had been boarded up for many years. The doors were situated right next to the church's cornerstone, which dated back to the 1850s. On this special winter day, someone had placed a single red rose through the double doors' handles.

Why, Dale had no idea. Maybe it was a sign, reminding us of the power of unconditional love.

On another occasion, David was having lunch with a friend at a local restaurant. Upon receipt of the bill, he asked to use a pen in order to write a check for the meal. The waiter delivered a pen, the end of which was adorned with one beautiful oversized red silk rose.

David looked at the small pen with the large red rose attached to it, and the waiter commented, "People wouldn't think of stealing a red rose, the purest symbol of unconditional love."

These types of coincidences happened over and over during the creation of this story. We can only explain them as signs of encouragement from the Universe to continue writing, knowing that all is in order.

This novel is about discovering one's place in the world and finding that life sometimes takes you 180 degrees from where you thought you were headed. We invite you to discover your place on this Earth, fully enjoying the adventure each step of the way.

May the puzzle of your life fit together like a magnificent masterpiece, woven with experiences that build strong character and integrity.

We encourage you to discover the unconditional love, wisdom, and insight presented in **GIFT OF THE SOUL** and wish you all the best on your life's journey to self-discovery.

With Unconditional Love,

—Dale Colclasure

—David Jensen

PS: Remember, in life we have three responsibilities:

1) To be who we are and to share that with others;

2) To follow our dreams; and

3) To love.

One

Spring—about one month prior to my graduation from college. I was seated in a program planning class at the University of Colorado in Boulder. I needed the course in order to fulfill my final graduation requirements. And then, after graduation, I would be on my way to achieving a lifelong dream, that of owning a health club.

We had just received our final papers back. The topic of my paper was “The Best Health Club.” I had completed some extensive research into area health clubs. I distributed questionnaires, talked with owners, members, and staff, and had asked for their feedback as to what problems they observed in their existing facilities and what suggestions they had for improving their clubs. I then compiled the results and suggestions into a paper.

I received the seemingly nonexistent “A” on my paper and a comment from the professor, Donald Zempler.

“Don’t think you’re so smart.”

I was the only student in class to receive an “A.” Zempler was not one to give many “A’s” or exams. His gift to our class of promising graduates was to free us of a final exam and replace it with speaking visits from three extremely successful local business people. At that time, I had no idea that this was to be the beginning of a spiritual journey for me.

Our first visitor was Donna Horton. She was the owner of one of the largest consulting firms in the state. The major thing I remember from her presentation was that she was about to give up on her business after only one year because of a lack of clients. Then a friend stepped in and offered her some financial assistance. This loving act allowed Donna to keep her business open. After only three years, her company became one of the most prominent and well respected firms in the state. She and her company were now known as national leaders in the consulting arena.

During our next class, the guest speaker was Tom Whitiker. Tom was a tall, slender man with an extremely deep voice. He was the owner and manager of a restaurant formerly named "The Stable Stop." He purchased the dying restaurant with dreams of turning it around. It was in a great location, in a high-traffic area, near the college campus. It had plenty of parking but not many customers since its opening four years prior.

Tom completed a feasibility study with the assistance of some successful local restaurant owners. He discovered that no one liked the old name, so he changed it. He also discovered that the previous owners never advertised, so he began a strategic advertising campaign.

The inside of the restaurant looked extremely dull, and so he remodeled it with an array of unique items that were characteristic of Boulder. His methods of remodeling were unlike any that I had ever heard of. He put a sign on the men's rest room that pointed to the women's and vice versa. He had tables and chairs mounted on the ceiling and light fixtures coming out of the floors. He did many similar kooky things throughout the entire restaurant.

The wait staff was allowed to wear whatever they wanted, and they never served the same table twice; they just rotated. So you didn't really know who worked there, who was waiting on you, or who was a customer.

The staff all pooled their tips and divided them evenly. All of this was part of the restaurant's "confusing" new gimmick. It was one that also challenged your mind. Tom said that his restaurant was something "to experience" and it was. The restaurant became one of the most successful in town, especially among the college population. And since there were nearly 30,000 students attending the university, the restaurant began to flourish. Tom's final thought was to remind us that his restaurant's success didn't come about without the help of others.

He left us by saying, "You can accomplish anything in life with a dream, some creativity, and a little help from others."

The two speakers thus far had truly been a gift from Professor Zempler.

I was working part time at a local health club and was hoping to land a job there permanently after graduation. I worked the reception area at Peak East Athletic Club. My job consisted of taking membership cards, greeting individuals, and handing people clean towels. I was informed when I started that I had the most important job in the club because I was the first person that a guest would see when they entered the facility, and this set the tone for their entire visit. I agreed with this, and at age twenty-one, was ready to take on the business world and to find my place in it as soon as possible. The owner had also hinted that they would probably take me on full time after I graduated.

I was only weeks away from graduation, and although this was a step closer to my dream, I also had a lot of studying to do in preparation for my final exams. So I took my books to work and studied during the evening shift.

One night, I was studying for the final exam in my animal behavior class, an elective that I had chosen to take for an easy "A." It turned out to be anything but easy. With an "A" on the final, I had hoped for a "C" in the class. I was reading about brown bears and how they try to charge anything that stands in their path. It was interesting to discover that, if you stand up to the brown bear when it charges and show no fear, the bear will retreat. I found this a fascinating and yet worthless piece of information, which had no place in my life whatsoever. But, the possibility of a "brown bear" question being on the final the next day did exist.

That same evening, an individual approached the front desk. I didn't see him because I was reading about brown bears. I heard the man clear his throat, and I looked up immediately and smiled. It was a club member, an older gentleman, carrying a racquetball racket.

"I sure wish my jobs growing up would have paid me to do homework."

His delivery didn't seem at all threatening. His face was unexpressive for a moment, and I wasn't sure how to respond. I didn't know this member's name and had never seen him in the club before. I had been caught doing school work and thought that my next move could determine the fate and possible future of my job. I was about to apologize when the gray-haired man extended his arm and smiled.

"William J. Gustafson. Call me Bill."

Relieved, I stood up, and put my hand out.

"Drew, Drew Wilson. I'm sorry." We shook hands. Bill smiled again, which put me at ease.

"I think I'd be on the phone with my girlfriend if I worked back there all night," he said winking at me.

I smiled back, wondering why I'd never seen him before.

"I travel quite a bit and usually only get in here during the day," Bill said, answering my unspoken question.

Bill headed back towards the racquetball courts. I sat down to study once again, but for some reason was unable to do so.

I sat at the front desk for the rest of the evening contemplating what Bill had said about being on the phone with a girlfriend. I was gay and hadn't seriously dated a girl since my first year in college. I was attracted to men but didn't share that bit of information often. I had always passed as a heterosexual and led a somewhat discouraging life when it came to the dating scene. Being involved in the sports community, I thought that if it ever got out that I was gay it would destroy my career and my dream of ever owning my own health club. So I just pretended to be busy or not interested. It was lonely at times.

I grew up in a family that never talked about sex. My father and mother both worked. I had two older brothers. Our family wasn't very close. When I was young, my grandmother would watch me after school until my brothers or parents got home.

My oldest brother, Frank, used to call me "fairy" a lot. He always had girlfriends and loved to tell me the most intimate details of his sexual encounters with them. When it didn't get any reaction out of me, he would call me a "fairy."

My other brother, Jarred, would see good looking women and point them out to me. "Drew, don't you just love women's bodies?"

I didn't know how to respond. I liked women. I had a lot of girls interested in me, but I didn't share the same physical attraction. Since I wasn't sexually attracted to females, I would just remain quiet when Jarred asked the question. I became more withdrawn from dating women as time went on and didn't date a single female my senior year in college.

The day after I met Bill, we were to have speaker number three in Zempler's class. As the man walked into the class, I looked up from my desk. It was Bill. I was surprised. It's strange when coincidental things happen in life. I meet him for the first time the previous night, and then suddenly here he is speaking to our class.

Zempler introduced Bill to the class. Bill scanned the front row and winked at me. I felt privileged. I really had no idea what Bill did for a living or what he was going to talk about. I assumed that he was retired. Bill told the class that he had sold cars for twenty-seven years at a local car dealership. When he retired, he was considered the best car salesman in the state and had received many sales awards. He now traveled the world speaking, consulting, and working with nonprofit organizations. He went almost everywhere he was asked to speak.

Bill told us he was seventy-five years old. He sure didn't look it. I was surprised that someone seventy-five would even have enough energy to get out of bed and tie their shoes, but Bill was different. He had a sensational spark about him. If given the choice, this was the type of man that almost everyone would pick for a grandfather.

Bill spoke about his life. He had met a girl named Nancy Billings, when he was fifteen. They fell in love and were married at age sixteen. They had raised four children and were still very happily married. Nancy had never worked outside the home and was happy being at home or traveling on occasion with Bill.

Bill told the class, towards the end of his presentation, "In this life we have two responsibilities.

"First: To find out who it is that we are and then to share that with others.

"Second: To discover what it is that we love to do and then go do it."

Bill said that this simple formula was the key to a happy life. And, ending his speech, he said, **"And last of all, to love.** We must first love ourselves and everything about ourselves. Then, and only then, can we truly love others. You see, I lied. We really have three responsibilities in life: **To be, to dream, and to love."**

He explained that when he first started speaking, the salesmen he spoke to would leave the room when he talked about love. They just wanted to know how to sell more cars. So he would concentrate on the first two responsibilities and then throw in the third at the end of his speeches. It worked out much better that way. Bill told us that he had lived his entire life based on these three responsibilities and found them to be essential to a happy and fulfilling life.

Bill was much different from the previous two speakers. He seemed to speak not only about career but also about our place in the world. This touched me and everyone in the class. He was the only speaker to receive a standing ovation.

Two

The night before graduation, I had a strange dream.

I dreamed that I was flying. Not in a plane or any other mechanical device. I was flying freely above the Earth. I moved between the stars and planets. I felt so free and content. It all seemed so real to me. I encircled the Earth.

I awoke to the sound of my alarm clock, feeling slightly dizzy. It was strange. I had never had a dream like that in my entire life but felt it had a significance yet unknown to me.

I sat through the entire graduation ceremony daydreaming about what Bill had said to our class only weeks before. His talk turned out to be the commencement address that I was supposed to hear, because I had no idea who gave ours or what they said.

The day after graduation, I was offered a full-time position at the health club. I liked it there and was happy with the offer. One day after graduation, and already I had a permanent job at a place that I liked and was involved in a career that I loved. I felt very blessed.

Within a month, I was promoted to assistant membership coordinator. My job wasn't much different than before. I still spent most of my time at the front desk, but now I gave tours of the facility, too. I even received a new name tag, and I was able to work the daytime hours that I preferred.

My boss and club owner, Janet Strong, and I had a long discussion regarding my plans for the future. She asked me where I wanted to be, professionally, in the next five years. I didn't know what it was about, being out of college and moving on through life, but it seems as if everything changes. I wasn't sure where I wanted to be in five years. I had some feelings of fear surface when I thought about the future. I knew I didn't want to be stuck behind the front desk of a health club, but I refrained from sharing that with Janet.

One day at work, I found myself thinking about Bill. I hadn't seen him in awhile. I began to think about his life and wondered if he had always known his path in life or if it just shaped itself as time went on. Bill seemed to be one of the very few people I knew who was 100% content with his life—not just some of the time, all of the time.

I tried to talk to a few people at work about Bill. They either didn't really know who I was talking about or didn't seem to care. Steve, a new front desk employee, said that he knew who Bill was and thought that he may have been in one evening recently. Steve said that he was too busy reading when the member came in to make a positive identification.

An entire month went by. I was liking my new job—not loving it, but liking it. Then an opportunity presented itself to me. Janet was unable to attend a fitness conference in San Diego, California, because she had a special family member visiting at the time. She asked if I would like to attend the conference in her place. Three other employees from the club were going, and I was next in line to attend if I so wanted. I thought it would be a great experience, so I accepted the offer. I would be able to bond with a few club employees and spend a couple of summer days in beautiful San Diego. I found out that I would be attending the weekend conference with Donna, the aerobics coordinator, Monica, the fitness coordinator, and Keith Johnson, the weight room manager.

Keith and I would be sharing a room, which made me slightly uncomfortable. Keith was an extremely attractive guy. I found that, on occasion, I would discover myself staring at him. I did my job at work, but didn't socialize a great deal with anyone there because I didn't want them to discover I was gay. I thought if they knew, it would be detrimental to my job.

I remembered an incident that involved this guy, John, whom I swam with when I was in high school. There were rumors about his sexuality. John was a quiet guy. People used to call him a "fag" and pick on him. He ended up dropping off the swim team. And soon after that, he and his family moved away. I never knew why but definitely had my suspicions.

We arrived at the conference on Friday night and checked in at the hotel. I was really nervous about being in the same room as Keith. I knew he wasn't married, but I didn't think he was gay.

We all went out to dinner immediately after checking in to the hotel. The conference was to begin the next morning, and so we decided to dine at a restaurant located near the hotel.

After dinner, we walked down near the ocean. It was a beautiful evening. As we were walking, I heard what I thought to be a familiar voice off in the near distance. A man and a woman were seated on a bench a short way ahead of us laughing and carrying on. It looked like Bill. I approached cautiously, thinking that no way would this be possible. Donna, Monica, and Keith continued on. I told them that I would meet them back at the hotel. I moved in behind Bill and the much smaller woman. Just as I was about to speak, Bill turned around. It was as if he sensed my presence.

"Hey, Bill," I said.

He smiled and then rose to greet me. Bill introduced me to his wife, Nancy. She was a beautiful, slightly gray-haired, older woman—everything I would have imagined his wife to be. They invited me to sit with them and watch the sun set behind the ocean. I sat with Bill and Nancy for about an hour talking and laughing. They told me about how they had met, about their wonderful children, and about their life together. They seemed to be like two young kids in love. It was amazing that they had been together almost sixty years and still had this amazing spark between them. I asked Bill what their secret was.

"Unconditional love," Bill said simply and then smiled at Nancy. She leaned over and kissed him on the cheek. I was so inspired by their relationship and realized it was something I wanted in my own life. My parents had never shown each other this kind of affection. Bill and Nancy's relationship had such a gentleness to it.

I looked at my watch. It was getting late. "I need to get back to the hotel," I said.

"You should stop by my office when you get back in Boulder," Bill said, as he stood up. "I'll be back in town on Monday."

"Okay," I said. "We're all getting back Monday morning. Anytime after that works for me."

I left, filled with the infectious joy and tranquility that Nancy and Bill possessed, and made my way back to the hotel.

I got back to the hotel room and opened the door, only to find Keith and Donna in bed together.

"Close the fucking door!" Keith yelled.

I was shocked. I moved quickly out of the room and closed the door behind me. I spent the entire night in the hallway waiting for Donna to leave the room. She never did. Consequently, I didn't get a lot of sleep and wasn't at my best for the conference the next day.

The following day, we attended a few management seminars and then had some free time. I didn't want to be around my coworkers after the previous evening's exchange. Here I was, in a beautiful city, doing what I thought I wanted to do for the rest of my life, and yet, it didn't feel right.

I enjoyed staying fit (swimming, running, lifting weights) and being around fit people, yet the more I was around my coworkers, the less I wanted to be around them. *These were fit people, but were they healthy?* I wasn't sure.

I decided to spend more of my time alone in San Diego. I was still upset that I had had to spend the entire night in the hallway. Keith pulled me aside during a morning break and apologized for his behavior. He assured me that it wouldn't happen again.

The agenda for Sunday, the final day of the seminar, was a wrap-up with some prominent fitness professionals and then a featured keynote speaker. I noticed on the program that Bill was the keynote speaker. Wow! I wouldn't have missed his talk for the world.

Bill spoke about the fitness industry and where the trends seemed to be going, but then he addressed what he saw as a problem within not only the fitness world but the corporate world as well.

"As we progress through this new millennium, we seem to be moving towards the total annihilation of service to our fellow human beings. Our computerized, voice-mailed, worldwide-webbed existence has made things much easier, yes, but in this, we are creating more and more distance between ourselves and our fellow humans."

I wasn't sure exactly where Bill was going with his talk, but he had captivated the entire room. The intensity of his voice commanded attention.

"We, the fitness professionals of today, are in our clubs to guide and instruct people about how to take care of themselves. And you club owners and managers are here to help get some insight into keeping the dollars flowing in and the doors open to your great clubs. The best way to keep those dollars rolling in is to make sure that our clubs promote not only fitness, but health and wellness. And this starts with our staff. We cannot expect our staff to treat anyone who enters the doors of our facilities better than *we* treat *them*. We need to step back and appreciate those who work for us. So many times, I see the exact opposite. I challenge all of us here today to put the focus on loving and appreciating our family of employees, and they in turn will pass that on to the club guests. Quality will always outperform quantity in the long run, if you give it a chance."

It seemed that the employees sure enjoyed his speech. I'm not sure that the club owners were on the same page, until Bill delivered his concluding thoughts. He spoke of his workdays.

"I sold cars for twenty-seven years. I was fired from three car dealerships. Why? Because I wouldn't pressure the sale. I was interested in working hand in hand with my coworkers, getting to know my customers, and giving them exactly what it was they were looking for. If it wasn't at our dealership, I would send them to another. My first three bosses didn't appreciate this and sent me to the other dealerships. I finally found a dealer/owner who was willing to try the very philosophy that I preach to you today. He allowed us to work together, to be ourselves, to be honest, and to do what most of us loved. Yes, I led many a customer right to another dealership if that meant they got what they wanted. But what I was doing was building an invisible customer base. You see, maybe they did walk out the door. Maybe they didn't buy from me. But many of those people, the same ones that didn't buy cars from me, referred others to our dealership and to me specifically. And boy, did they buy!

"Folks, we are all in the people business, everyone on this planet. It doesn't matter if we sell cars, mop floors, manage clubs, or sell hamburgers. We are all here to give the best of ourselves and we do that by extending ourselves in service to others, by going the extra mile. I went on to be one of the most successful salesmen in the entire western United States.

"I would like you all to understand something. If we love ourselves first, we can then love others. Again, we are all in the people business. I know that when I have the opportunity to interact with another individual, I can make that an experience for both of us to benefit from. I believe that is the reason we are all here on this big planet—to connect. When we truly connect with another, giving our best, from the heart, amazing things happen.

"I offer you all this challenge. Go back to your clubs and start to do things differently. Help each other out, go the extra mile, treat your staff like gold. They will then turn your club into gold. Your club will be the talk of the town. Not that it's a place people just go to get fit, but a place where people go to be better people, healthier people. Thank you. Thank you for allowing me this time in your life."

The room was quiet for a few moments and then people began to stand up and clap. I think that I was one of the first ones standing. Bill received another standing ovation! This seemed to happen to him often. He had quite a different approach, and boy was it effective. I moved up to the front of the room and thanked him for speaking. Bill thanked me for listening, which made me feel great.

During our last day in San Diego, my coworkers decided to check out the stores in nearby La Jolla. I declined the invitation to join them and, instead, decided to walk along the beach.

I walked barefoot in the sand. It was so peaceful walking along the beach listening to the waves crash upon the Earth. The portion of beach that I walked on appeared to be desolate that day. I took the time to reflect on Bill's talk. It had been so uplifting. Then I started to run along the beach with a newfound energy. I felt connected to the Earth and sea as I ran.

I noticed a man seated alone on a rock formation a short way ahead of me. As I neared the rocks, I saw that, once again, it was Bill. How odd, I thought, *A man I hardly know from the same town as me keeps appearing in my life over and over, and now in a place where neither one of us lives.* The strangeness of these coincidental meetings finally sank in. I approached Bill. "Hello."

He looked up and smiled.

I slipped my shoes on and made my way up onto the rocks. "What are you doing?"

Bill closed a small notebook that he had been writing in. "Just putting a few thoughts down on paper. I like to stay connected."

I wasn't exactly sure what Bill was talking about, but it didn't matter. "Where's Nancy?" I asked.

"We take time away from each other now and then. Nancy loves to shop, and I do not."

"Do you wonder why we keep running into each other, Bill?" I was speaking to the obvious.

"Because we're supposed to," Bill said as he smiled, looking directly at me.

"What do you mean?" wrinkling my forehead.

Bill moved down off the rocks, and I followed.

"You have to admit, it's pretty weird," I said.

"You're my student."

"Yeah?"

I wasn't sure if I was ready for this. Bill chuckled and then proceeded to talk as we walked along the beach. "It may sound rather cliché, but haven't you ever heard the expression, 'When the student is ready, the teacher appears'?"

I had not. Bill smiled as we continued to walk. He didn't say much but reminded me to stop by his office when I arrived back in Boulder.

I made my way back to the hotel room. Keith was just finishing a shower when I opened the door.

He came out of the bathroom, and I turned to him and noticed that he was stark naked. He had a beautiful, chiseled body. I couldn't help but stare. I knew that he noticed my staring, yet he didn't say anything right away. I tried to turn away, but all I could do was look at him. It was as if my body was in control of me. Keith reached for a towel and began to dry his blonde hair, and then his body.

"So, where've you been?" he asked.

I regained control of my body, fidgeting a bit. "At the beach."

"Cool."

This small interchange was followed by a momentary silence.

"So, are you gay?" he said.

I didn't say a thing; my face said it all.

"Hey, it's cool if you are and all. I just noticed you were staring at me."

I felt my mouth drop to the floor, and I was unable to speak.

Keith dropped the towel, moved naked across the room, grabbed his underwear, and continued to dress. "Well, you better get ready for dinner. I told the girls that I'd drag you out with us tonight."

We smiled at each other, and Keith came over and patted me on the shoulder. "I'm sorry again, about the other night with Donna. It wasn't very cool of me. You're a good guy, Drew."

I still couldn't speak, but knew now after a second apology, that Keith was sincere. Amazing how he had sized up the true me in only a few moments. I didn't have to say a word and yet felt accepted. I changed my shirt and then we headed off to join the girls.

The dinner, our last meal in San Diego, was extremely nice. I had some of the best seafood I can ever remember eating. We ate at a restaurant that overlooked the ocean. Our waiter was blonde and very attractive. He possessed that shimmering hair swimmers get in chlorinated pools. Keith kept looking at me and raising his eyebrows every time the waiter passed. The girls didn't know what to think and were more interested in finding out what I had been doing by myself all day.

During dinner, I was the only one in the group who wasn't drinking alcohol. Keith, Donna, and Monica were all drinking wine. I had seen firsthand how dangerous alcohol was because of my brother Frank's problems with it. I really didn't want to go down that road, so I just abstained from it entirely. I told the group about coincidentally meeting up with Bill yet again on the beach.

Monica was the only one to comment. “He sure is a nice man. I’ve seen him around the club.”

We finished our dinner and made our way back to the hotel after a short walk on the beach.

Three

Back in Colorado, I found that I was really looking forward to meeting with Bill again. I was also slightly nervous about being back at work, wondering whether Keith had told everyone around the club that I was gay. He hadn't. My opinion of Keith really changed after the trip. I had thought that he was this macho and insensitive guy, but I was wrong. He was really macho—macho and sensitive. This impressed me. The trip, all in all, had been a very positive experience, but I was glad to be home.

I called Bill's office that afternoon. Mary, Bill's assistant answered the phone. "Hello, Drew."

I hadn't even said a word. This was strange to me.

"Drew Wilson," I said.

"I had a feeling it was you. Sometimes it's kind of strange to people, but I've never been wrong when I get that feeling, so I just go with it," she said. "When would you like to come in and visit with Bill? I know that he is very excited to start working with you."

"He is?" I was surprised and perplexed as to why this man had taken such an interest in me and my life. I was also a bit frightened.

"How about next Monday, a week from today? Three o'clock?" she asked.

I agreed, hung up the phone, and went on with my life for the rest of the week.

The week seemed to pass rather slowly, and although I had some fear about meeting with Bill, I found myself excited as well. One day, Keith was standing at the front desk with me and a very attractive guy, near my age, came into the club. No other employees were around. After the guy moved away from the counter, Keith came over and elbowed me.

"So, what do you think of him?"

"I don't know." I was embarrassed. I looked around to see if anyone was watching.

"He's a good-looking guy. You're a good-looking guy."

I nodded and looked around again to see if

anyone was watching. I didn't know what else to do. Many thoughts went through my head. It was as if Keith was more comfortable with me being gay than I was. I began to wonder why he was so interested in trying to hook me up with a guy. I knew he wasn't gay. In fact, he and Donna were seeing each other now.

There was this aerobics instructor, Kimmy, that had started hanging around the front desk whenever I worked. Keith told me that she was interested in me, but I really hadn't picked up on her flirtatious actions until Keith pointed them out. It seemed so unnatural for me to notice that sort of thing with women. I didn't really want to deal with Kimmy, but she came up one day and asked me to go to a movie with her. I agreed. We decided to go that next Monday evening, the same day I was to visit with Bill.

Next Monday came. I arrived at Bill's office at exactly 3:00 p.m. The reception area was extremely modest, containing only a desk and a phone, a fish tank full of tropical fish, white couch and a water cooler. It was plain and peaceful.

Mary greeted me the minute I arrived. She was a sweet older woman, who looked to be about sixty. Her face glowed when she spoke. "You must be Drew?"

I smiled. It seemed strange to me that Mary had

no computer or even a notepad on her desk. She picked up on my thoughts.

"We believe in simplicity here."

I smiled again. The door to Bill's private office opened, and there stood Bill. The sun illuminated him from behind, giving his entire body an angelic glow, which was accentuated by his warm smile. I immediately felt at ease. It was as if he emitted unconditional love—the kind of feeling you have when you know everything is okay—a type of love I was not that familiar with at the time. Bill advanced and I stuck out my hand. He bypassed my hand and moved straight towards me, giving me a big hug.

"I've been looking forward to this day all week."

"Yes, he has," Mary smiled, nodding her head.

I felt as if I was a dignitary from another country that had finally been met by a longtime admirer.

Bill and I went to lunch. He took me to a health food store that had a small deli in the back. Bill told me that this place had some of the best and healthiest sandwiches around, and at very reasonable prices. Like Bill's office, this place was simple.

Why this place? I wondered to myself.

Bill told me that he had been coming to the deli for over twenty years.

We ordered a couple of sandwiches and then moved towards the cashier. Bill picked up a fresh red rose at the register. He didn't let me pay for the sandwiches. I focused on the rose, and I began to wonder. *Was Bill gay? Was the rose for me? Was it for Nancy? Maybe he was a dirty old man?*

We went outside and sat down at one of the two picnic tables situated in front of the store, under a large oak tree. We sat and ate in silence for a short while. I looked at the rose that Bill had propped up on the table.

"How's your sandwich?" Bill asked.

I anticipated something more from him.

"Good," I smiled reservedly. I was curious as to what this was all about and couldn't wait any longer.

As I was about to open my mouth, Bill spoke. "I know you have a lot of questions."

I did. I was beginning to feel very uncomfortable.

Bill spoke again. "The rose."

I swallowed. I didn't know why I was so bothered by the rose. I guess that the last thing I wanted to hear was that Bill was interested in me, sexually.

"The rose is the purest symbol of unconditional love," he said.

I swallowed but said nothing.

"I like to buy myself one now and then as a reminder."

Although I was relieved, I was also a bit surprised. I thought to myself, *This man buys flowers for himself?* I had never thought of doing such a thing. *Is he crazy?* We finished our sandwiches, and Bill suggested that we go for a short walk. We walked along a creek, near a small park across from the health food store.

"Drew, you are very special."

I was uncomfortable again.

"This may all seem very strange to you, but you have drawn me to you."

I didn't understand.

We continued to walk and Bill went on. "Life is much more than we really know."

"I'm feeling really uncomfortable."

Bill stopped, and so did I. He faced me.

"Why, Drew?"

I couldn't keep it back. It just came spilling out. "I'm gay." I had no control over what had just come out of my mouth. A rush of emotion had overcome me, and I had no way of holding it back. A few tears fell from my eyes, and I felt a sense of shame burst forth from my gut. Bill hugged me, while I cried in his arms. He said nothing, only held me. As my tears slowed, I pulled back from Bill. He handed me a handkerchief and smiled.

"What do you want from me?" I said, turning away in shame. Nothing like this had ever happened to me in my entire life. I couldn't explain exactly what I was feeling or what was happening.

"I want you to love yourself." Bill's simple words put me at ease.

I turned back to face him. "I'm sorry."

"You need not apologize for who you are, Drew."

"I don't know what just happened there," I said, wiping my eyes.

"It was a release. I do that occasionally."

"You do?"

"Tears are so very cleansing to the soul." Bill smiled at me and then looked at his watch, "We should probably be getting back."

I nodded in agreement.

When we arrived back at Bill's office, I started to head towards my car.

Bill called out to me. "Drew, I'd like you to do something, if you are willing."

I stopped and turned around, and Bill now stood in front of me.

"What?"

"Tonight, go home and take out a piece of paper. On it, I'd like you to write down everything that describes who you are as the person you see yourself to be. Don't question it, just start with the number one and see how many items you can come up with."

I thought for a minute. "Okay," I said.

"In a couple of days, call me or stop by the office. I'd like to see what you have come up with." Bill hugged me, and I hugged back this time.

As soon as I got back to work, I ran into Kimmy, who was just inside the door.

"Drew, could we reschedule for tonight?" she asked. "My father is coming into town for a business meeting that's scheduled for tomorrow. The only time we can spend together is this evening. He wants to take me out to dinner."

"Sure." I was relieved at this sudden change in plans. I wanted to spend some time alone and work on the assignment that Bill had suggested to me.

"How about tomorrow night?" she asked.

I agreed and noticed Keith was watching our interaction from behind the front desk.

Kimmy quickly kissed my cheek and then moved away. "Thanks Drew."

Keith strolled over after Kimmy left and placed his hand on my shoulder. "She likes you."

I knew that, but having him point it out made me uncomfortable.

"Don't lead her on, man."

I wrinkled my forehead, and Keith continued. "This is a cool club, Drew. I don't think people really care who dates who, if ya know what I mean."

I thought that he was trying to tell me that it was okay being openly gay, but the thought of letting that fact out was extremely frightening. I didn't want to lead anyone on, but I was also afraid of losing my job should anyone discover my secret.

I went directly home after work to my small apartment. I grabbed a bite to eat and then sat down at the kitchen table with a legal pad. With pen in hand, I began the list—the list that described who I thought I was. The first thing that I put on the list was 1) fitness consultant. Next, I listed my physical attributes: 2) six feet tall; 3) dark hair; 4) one-hundred-seventy pounds; 5) green eyes; 6) muscular; 7) athletic; 8) nice teeth. Then I stopped. I wasn't sure what I should list next.

I looked at the pad of paper for a short while. Then a wave of personal identifiers flowed through, most concerning my family: 9) son; 10) brother; 11) cousin. Then I listed my sports identifiers: 12) soccer player; 13) swimmer; 14) runner; 15) weight lifter; 16) skier; 17) snow boarder.

After about an hour, I had listed nearly one hundred descriptors—things that I associated with who I was. The very last thing that I put on the list was item 101) a gay man. This was the most difficult item to write down. It was the one thing that I didn't feel good about listing. I noticed how exhausted I was after I had completed the list. I wasn't sure why. So I went to bed.

The next day, I phoned Bill from work during a break. Mary answered, once again knowing that it was me before I said anything.

"Drew, I'm sorry but Bill has gone to Boston for a speaking engagement. He told me if you called to give you his hotel phone number and to let you know that he probably wouldn't be in much, but that you should feel free to leave a message."

I thanked Mary and took down the number, deciding to call Bill during my lunch break.

I took Keith with me to lunch. We went to the same health food store and deli that Bill had taken me to the previous day. During lunch, I excused myself from the table and tried to call Bill from the store's pay phone. There was no answer, so I left Bill a message.

"Hey, Bill, this is Drew. I made the list like you asked me to, and I have one hundred and one things on it. Have fun in Boston." I hung up and went back to join Keith at the picnic table.

"Who'd ya call? Someone special?" Keith asked.

"No," I shook my head.

"Hey, I think you should ask that cute guy out at the club. He likes you."

"How do you know that?"

"Drew, I'm the love god of the club. I know these things." Keith chuckled, and I started laughing.

At that point, I really felt that my friendship with him was something solid, and I was surprised at what I said next. "Hey Keith, how come you're so cool with me being gay?"

Keith finished chewing a bite of his sandwich and then swallowed. "My brother *was* gay."

"Was?"

Keith smiled, then looked up to the sky and then back to me.

"Todd, yeah. He was four years older than me. I remember him telling the whole family at the dinner table when he was like twelve years old that he was gay. He was a great guy. My mom was cool with it. My dad, well, it took a while for him to accept. I think Dad thought that it was his fault or something, but Todd was such a great person that my dad soon got over it. Todd was a jock—no one thought he was gay.

He had a boyfriend, Larry. Larry moved back home to Montana after he found out that he had cancer—in the brain—a tumor. It was really bad. Well, Todd drove up there to visit him and on the way back—" Keith stopped talking.

I swallowed.

"He fell asleep at the wheel, died instantly, they say." Keith's eyes teared up, then he smiled as he wiped a tear from his cheek. "You kinda remind me of Todd. He was really a cool guy. I didn't care that he was gay."

"I'm sorry about your brother," I said.

"We'd better get back to work."

We drove back to the club, not talking too much—a few glances back and forth at each other accompanied by a few smiles, but nothing verbal. I felt extremely honored that Keith was comfortable enough with me to open up his heart about something that seemed so painful. I didn't say anything about it, but I think he knew how I felt. We arrived back at the club, and the workday continued.

Four

That evening, I had my date with Kimmy. We went to a movie, and afterward, I couldn't even remember what movie we had just seen. All I could think about the entire night was that I had to tell her that I was gay. I didn't know how to go about it or when was the best time to tell her. I'm sure she sensed my mental absence during the entire date. We decided to get ice cream after the movie. I became more and more quiet as the evening progressed. I was waiting for just the right moment to tell her my secret. The right moment never arrived.

Seated at a table in the ice cream parlor, I finally said something very quickly, between bites of ice cream. "Wow, what a movie. How's your ice cream?

I'm gay. So, what do you want to do now? How about bowling?" I thought if I strung enough thoughts and questions together she wouldn't hear me or she would be so disgusted that she would just leave.

What she said surprised me. "I thought you might be, but I wasn't sure. Let's."

"Huh?" I said.

"Sure. Let's go bowling."

How cool, I thought. My worst fears were being erased right in front of me. An evening full of inner turmoil melted in an instant by a simple comment. "Sure, let's go bowling." I gained a new respect for Kimmy that evening.

I drove Kimmy home after we finished bowling, and she leaned over and gave me a kiss on the cheek before she got out of my car.

"Drew, you're a sweet man; thank you for a great evening."

Kimmy just wanted a friendship. She was a beautiful girl, and although I wasn't attracted to her sexually, I *was* attracted to her spirit.

I arrived home to a message from Bill waiting on my answering machine. "Drew, hello, this is Bill. I'm still here in Boston. I'll be back in Boulder tomorrow evening. One hundred and one things on your list, that's great! I'd love to hear about your experience with the exercise. Why don't we get together for lunch the day after tomorrow. Take care, friend. Bye." Bill's message was the perfect nightcap for a growth-filled evening.

I went to work the next morning, and I noticed a meeting was ending with Janet Strong and a few of the managers. Janet approached me and asked if we could speak privately. I immediately went into fear mode, thinking that they had just completed a meeting about me and that Kimmy must have told them I was gay. I was afraid they were going to fire me. I took in a deep breath, swallowed, and then made my way into Janet's office.

"Drew, close the door please," were Janet's first words.

I closed the door and moved over to sit in a chair across from Janet.

Janet looked directly at me and spoke. "Drew, there is something I would like to discuss with you." My heart sank, as she continued. "I ran into Professor Zempler at the university yesterday ... "

I was relieved.

"He informed me that you completed some type of a study on health clubs last semester and also wrote quite an impressive paper about your findings. I'd love to talk to you about it. I know the conference was beneficial to all of you in San Diego. I would like our club to be 'the best' in every respect. I enjoy having you here. Your work is impressive, the members love you, and so do the staff. I think we may be able to use some of your valuable ideas, and I'd like to hear them." Janet paused for a moment, then said, "I would also like to give you a raise."

I felt a smile expand across my face. How wrong I had been about this interaction. I had a real hang-up about being gay. I told Janet that I would be happy to bring my paper in and discuss it with her.

Thursday arrived, and I was very excited to have lunch with Bill. I brought sandwiches. Bill had a meeting in Denver early in the afternoon, so we ate at his office. Bill's private office consisted of two couches, an end table, and a telephone—no desk. Simple, similar to the reception area. He had an exceptional view of the Boulder Flatirons, a breathtaking arrangement of Rocky Mountain peaks. I handed my list of personal identifiers to Bill and stopped eating while he scanned them.

He looked through the sheets of paper for about ten minutes without saying a word. He then handed them back to me and smiled. "Why did you list being gay last?"

"I don't know." I was lying.

"I don't believe you wanted to list being gay at all ... "

He was right.

"And I think that if I asked you to do this again you would probably come up with five hundred and one things."

"Probably," I said.

Bill patted my knee, then stood up. "Drew, being gay is such a small part of who you are. I think you make it bigger than it needs to be."

"I know I do."

He then told me I needed to treasure my uniqueness and that my list was just the beginning of my recognition of that uniqueness.

"We are all diamonds in the rough, unique in our individual expressions. Each of us needs to cherish and appreciate ourselves more."

I truly agreed. Bill's wise words made me think about the items I had listed. The gift in this exercise was that I did start to see how *all* of the items made me, me, not just one or two of them.

"Do you realize that in this lifetime there will never be anyone else exactly like you on this entire planet? Your uniqueness is truly a gift, one to be cherished," Bill said.

I contemplated silently what Bill had just asked, and I felt a new warmth inside.

"Are you ready for your next assignment?" he asked.

Five

I was excited to find out what my next assignment would be. I stood up and faced Bill. "Sure, lay it on me."

"I would like you to perform five good deeds, anonymously, within the next week."

"Okay." This seemed like a great assignment, and I listened as Bill explained things for me in more depth.

"You may choose whatever it is you feel qualifies as a 'good deed,' but you cannot tell anyone about any of the deeds, who it was for, or what it was. If you do this, it will not count."

I agreed without question, and Bill smiled and looked down at his watch. "I'm off to Cleveland for the week, and we'll touch base when I get back in town."

Bill gave me a warm hug before I left his office. I began to think about how much better I felt about myself since my first encounter with this loving soul. I was enjoying the journey.

The next day, I was committed to complete my first good deed. I had never really done anything like this before and wasn't sure what to do or how to begin, or what really constituted a "good deed."

I was working and had to go to the post office during my lunch break to mail a few bills and pick up my mail. I thought maybe something would present itself to me that would qualify as my first good deed.

At the post office, I parked behind a black Honda Civic exactly like mine, except for the fact that this one had a New Mexico license plate. I went into the post office, which was extremely busy, retrieved my mail from my post office box, dropped off some letters, and left the building.

Outside the post office, as I was walking back to my car, I noticed a few envelopes lying on the ground next to where the black Honda with the New Mexico plate had been parked. My curiosity was sparked, so I bent down to retrieve the envelopes. They appeared to be three unmailed bills all containing a New Mexico return address but no name. What most caught my attention, though, was the fact that all of these envelopes were without any postage. Several thoughts flashed through my mind. *If these payments are not received by the companies, the person who is sending them may be charged a late fee or maybe even have their accounts closed. This person probably had no idea that the payments would not be received by the companies on time, and it could be several weeks before they even find this out. Maybe this person was traveling and just needed to make a stop at the post office to mail the bills.*

Here was my answer staring me right in the face. I clutched the envelopes firmly in my hand, marched back into the post office, walked up to the counter, and bought three first-class stamps. I affixed them to the envelopes and dropped them into the outgoing mail slot, wishing them well on their journey. My good deed number one was complete. This was a simple good deed and a good start. I felt a sense of warmth inside afterwards. As Bill had suggested, I told no one about what I had done.

The next day arrived, and I was committed to perform good deed number two. I was working the front desk at the health club entirely by myself that day because the majority of the front desk staff were attending a training class in Denver. In walked the gorgeous guy that Keith had been nudging me towards. I realized I was slightly nervous to see him. I had never greeted him before, and hence, didn't know his name. Our club prided itself on knowing the members' names, and I did know most of them. I think I had avoided this guy because I felt an attraction toward him. This was compounded by my own lack of comfort with my sexuality. And, adding kindling to the fire, I wasn't even sure if he was gay or not. My mind raced as this guy approached the front desk. Keith told told me that he always worked out alone and seemed rather quiet. I smiled as he approached the counter.

"Hello. My name is Drew. I haven't met you before." I put my hand out. I think it was shaking slightly, I was so nervous. The gentlemen looked at me and, with half a smile, stuck his hand out. "Rod."

We shook hands. His was as cold as mine. I stared at him for a moment, loosened my grip, and then took his membership card, handed him a towel, and watched as he moved away. He turned back just before rounding the corner. Rod had a muscular build, was about my height, and had dark hair and beautiful blue eyes. I think my palm was sweating at that point. I watched him until he was out of sight. I was to meet with Janet regarding my study of health clubs a bit later, so I spent the next hour reviewing my college paper. Part of my mind was also on the lookout for what might be the next deed I was to perform.

After reviewing my paper on successful health clubs, Janet and I walked around the club. She looked through my paper as I discussed the contents, and I made a few suggestions for changes at the club. I had discovered through my research that one of the main ingredients for a highly successful fitness facility was ensuring that the members feel appreciated on a continuous basis. This means much more than simply collecting their membership dues every month. The staff needs to take the time to get to know them and learn a little about them. The biggest compliment the successful clubs I researched had been given was that the staff knew the members' names. Our club was pretty good in this area, but there was room for improvement.

As Janet and I walked around, I was able to address every member by their name, except one. We walked upstairs to the weight room just as we were discussing the name thing. Rod was moving towards the drinking fountain, and I approached him.

"Hey Rob, how's the workout going?"

"It's Rod," was his immediate response.

I smiled in embarrassment. I did know his name, but when I opened my mouth, something slightly different came out. Janet didn't say a word, but she smiled. She and I spent about four hours discussing my study and more suggestions that I had about how we could improve the club. In the back of my mind, I was still waiting for a situation to present itself to me, one in which I could perform my second good deed.

I went out to my car after work, feeling slightly exhausted, and I noticed a middle-aged woman standing on the median in the street that paralleled the club. She was holding a sign, soliciting help. She appeared to be homeless. I had never, prior to that moment, paid much attention to the homeless and had always thought that if I was able to get a job, so could they. But this time, as I looked at this woman, different thoughts about the homeless entered my mind. *What if she was unable to work because of a disability? What if she lost her job and couldn't find another one? What if she had a family to support? What if she had no family or friends? What if that was me someday?* The last thought frightened me. I knew then that something to do with this woman was to be my second good deed. But what? I thought for a few moments. I couldn't just go up and hand her money, because then she would know who gave it to her, and the deed wouldn't count. I watched her a bit longer.

Then, it came to me. There was a fast food restaurant next door. I went inside and purchased a hamburger, french fries, and a dessert, then inside the bag placed a ten dollar bill. Next, I thought about how I would deliver the bag without her knowing it. I couldn't ask someone to deliver it because then they would know about the good deed and it wouldn't count. Just as I pondered my dilemma, I noticed the woman had set her sign down next to her ragged jacket on the median and was making her way towards a gas station located on the corner.

I rushed closer and observed the woman move towards the gas station's rest room. This was my opportunity to deliver the bag. After she entered the rest room, I quickly ran to the median and placed the bag on her jacket next to her sign, which read, "Please Help," followed by, "Thank you." I then ran back to the fitness club parking lot and quickly jumped into my car. I sat there and watched, my heart pounding.

After a few moments, the woman came out of the rest room, and crossed the street, making her way back to her humble perch. She immediately picked up the small bag, opened it, and pulled out the hamburger, which she devoured along with the french fries in what seemed like seconds. She then looked back into the bag, pulled out the ten dollar bill, and smiled, revealing her broken teeth. She wadded up the bill and stuck it in her pants pocket. She then wrapped the paper bag around the dessert and placed it ever so carefully inside her jacket.

She picked up her sign, and with a newfound energy, smiled and waved to the passing cars. I don't know if it was what I had done that brought this apparent new sense of hope to this woman or if it was something else, but, witnessing the event, I felt joy at having committed this personal act of unconditional love.

The next day arrived and with it my opportunity to seek out and perform good deed number three. Once again, I had no clue as to what good deed I would perform this day. It was my day off from the club, and I hadn't made any specific plans. A thought quickly entered my mind. *What if I drove to Denver and offered to help out at one of the homeless shelters for the day?*

I didn't have a clue where the thought came from but it sounded like an undertaking that would be an adventure. Watching that woman on the street the day before definitely had affected my thoughts about homeless individuals. I wanted to do more for the homeless.

I drove the thirty minutes to Denver, past a homeless shelter. I circled and drove around three times. There were approximately twenty homeless people standing outside the shelter entrance. The shelter was not located in the best part of town. I parked on a nearby side street. I was afraid of something, but I wasn't sure what. I sat in my car for about an hour before I had the nerve to get out. I did finally venture out from the safety of my automobile and made my way towards the shelter entrance. I approached the door and attempted to open it. It was locked.

An older homeless man approached me. "Not until five."

That was the extent of our interaction; he then walked away. The thought of going to the back door entered my mind. I quickly moved to the back and rang the delivery bell. After a few moments, the door opened. A sweet, robust woman, who looked to be in her early fifties, greeted me with a smile.

"I'm sorry, but we don't serve until five, dear."

"I'm not here for a meal. I would like to help you today," was my response.

"I'm Mandy." She smiled and held the door open. "Well, okay then."

As I walked inside, I noticed that about ten people were busy preparing a large feast. About six of them were around Mandy's age, I would guess. There was a woman there with her son. A priest or preacher was helping, and a very well-dressed businessman, minus his suit coat, was there among others.

Mandy introduced me to the group of volunteers. "Folks, this is ... "

"Drew," I said, completing her sentence. I received many smiles from the group, and then one of the older men, Hank, I believe was his name, waved me over.

"How's your potato-chopping arm?" he asked, holding up a knife as I moved in his direction.

"Pretty good, I think."

We were preparing the evening meal, which consisted of potato soup, fresh baked bread, salad, and cake. A local dairy donated individual cartons of milk daily to the shelter.

The time moved rather quickly, and I performed whatever task was asked of me throughout the day. A short time before we were to begin serving, I approached Hank, whom I had worked closest with most of the day and asked him a question. "Hank, why do you do this?"

"This must be the first time you've been here, son," he said, wrinkling his brow.

I wasn't exactly sure what to make of his answer, and I didn't have time to ask a follow-up question. Mandy had opened the front door and was directing homeless people toward the food line.

I was to dish up a serving of salad onto each individual's plate. There were probably two hundred people in line, waiting for a hot meal. The line was designed to move quickly. I began to scoop the salad on the people's plates as they moved past. I studied these folks as they went by. There were teenagers, mothers, sons, daughters, older folks, alcoholics, people of every ethnic origin one could imagine. These people represented a perfect slice of life. I believe that every single person for whom I scooped a serving of salad thanked me. These people thanked me for just putting a small amount of food on their plate during only one evening in time.

The line began to dwindle, and then I noticed someone familiar approaching from the end of the line. It was the homeless woman from Boulder that I had given the hamburger and money to the previous day. I was surprised to see her. I wondered how she had made her way from Boulder to Denver. A woman assisting her pulled her along through the line. I noticed that the Boulder woman had something in her hand. They arrived at my station in line. I asked the woman if she would like a helping of salad.

"She can't speak," her friend said.

I placed a serving of salad on her plate anyway, as well as dishing up one for her companion. A moment after they passed by, the homeless woman from Boulder turned back and threw something at me. The wadded piece of paper hit me and fell to the table.

Mandy witnessed the interaction that had just taken place and moved over to me, handing me the crumpled up paper.

"Drew, don't take it as an insult. The woman can't speak and usually writes something on a bag or napkin to give to one of the volunteers."

I took the paper and unfolded it. It was a paper bag from a fast foot restaurant, and written on the bag, in crayon, with childlike writing, were the words, "God bless you." I was deeply touched. How coincidental it was that I would receive that note. I wondered if she knew about the previous day and what I had done for her, but at the same time, I knew that she absolutely couldn't have.

I looked in her direction as she continued on through the line, giving me no further attention. I turned back to the service line and noticed that in my contemplative state, I had forgotten to place a serving of salad on the last individual's plate. He moved through the line anyway. I sought out a small serving plate and filled it with salad, then moved to where the man had seated himself, and set the salad down in front of him. Before I could move away the man grabbed my shirt and pulled me down to his level. He whispered in my ear with alcohol-laden breath, "You will do great things." He immediately let go and attacked the plate of food with his fork, paying me no further attention. I moved away.

There was enough food left over for the volunteers. Mandy told me that I should serve myself and find a place to sit among the people in the room and eat. I sat down with a newly homeless family. The husband had just lost his job the month prior, and they were now living on the streets and in local shelters, when there was room. His wife had the most pleasing smile.

"I am so grateful that you people are here," she said.

I was touched by this. They had a small boy who reminded me of myself as a child. He was cute, with green eyes, and he seemed so pure and wonderful. Even in the midst of their family crisis, he was able to let the spark of innocence shine through with laughter and wonder. I thought, *Kids have such a gift of using laughter to help diffuse even the most difficult situations in life.* I thanked them for letting me be in their lives for this short time and wished them the very best on their life's journey.

After I ate, I helped clean up and thanked Mandy for allowing me to be of service. She gave me a grand loving hug before I left the shelter.

As I drove back to Boulder, I thought about what Hank had said to me when I asked why he volunteered at the shelter. "This must be the first time you've been here," he'd said. Now I understood that this experience had enriched me in ways that I couldn't begin to describe in words. I thought about how much I wanted to share this experience with someone and then remembered what Bill had said. My good deeds would not count if I told anyone about them. I wondered why?

Six

The next day at the health club, a number of coworkers told me how happy I looked. Keith asked if I had gotten laid the previous night. I laughed. I felt so content and happy inside and credited the feelings to my previous days' experiences. I began to think about what I could do for good deed number four.

Once again, I had no idea what the deed would be that day, but I was sure that an opportunity would present itself. I was right. The club was slow that day for some unknown reason. We had a display rack in the front of the club where we would distribute flyers, free local papers, apartment guides, and other literature of interest. I had never really picked up anything from the rack to read, but did that day. I picked up the free local newspaper, the *Weekly Gazette,* and thumbed through it. As I did, I noticed a headline that read, “Gay Community Center Needs Help.” I read the article which explained how the local gay community center was extremely low on food for their client food bank. The food bank was for local individuals living with HIV and AIDS. I was surprised to read this. I had always thought that the Boulder community was one of the most affluent and giving communities. I then wondered if people were just not aware of the shortage. I didn’t even know that the community center had a food bank until I read the article. Then it hit me. This was to be my good deed number four. *What exactly?* I wasn’t sure as of yet. I brainstormed as my day continued and attempted to come up with a plan to help the community center.

A few hours later, I had some ideas and a plan. First, I would call the local radio station anonymously and ask the disc jockey if he/she had read the article. I then decided to write an anonymous letter to the editor of the local *Boulder Daily News* and voice my concerns about our community’s oversight in allowing something like this to happen. I titled my letter, “How could we let this happen?” I faxed the letter to the editor from a self-service fax machine located at a copy center near the health club. I then made a phone call to the local radio station from the pay phone outside of the club. I was on hold a short time while waiting to speak with the disc jockey, but I finally got through. The disc jockey said that he had seen the same story in the *Weekly Gazette* that morning but had only browsed over the article. He retrieved the paper while I was still on the phone. He agreed to mention the plight of the community center on the radio and even asked if I would like to discuss it "on air." I declined, but told the disc jockey that I would very much appreciate his mention of the center and the article. I told him that I wanted to remain anonymous and did not give him my name. I then hung up the phone and made my way back into the club.

Our club's sound system played the same local radio station that I had called. I turned up the volume slightly throughout the entire club in order to monitor the happenings on the air as the day progressed.

Within moments after I adjusted the volume, the disc jockey came on the air. "I received a call from an anonymous local listener regarding a small article in the *Weekly Gazette,* and I would like to read it to our listeners." He read the entire article over the air and then invited people to call in and discuss why they thought that something like this could happen in such a giving and supportive community. This was the beginning of a wonderful chain of events.

A manager from a local grocery store called in and agreed to have their store deliver twenty cases of canned goods to the community center before the day's end. That sparked another listener, a department store manager, to call and agree to have $500 worth of toiletries dropped off at the community center within the next few hours.

A few songs played and then a call came in from the editor of the daily paper who said that he had received a fax about the plight of the community center and would be writing an article to appear in the next morning's paper urging the people of the community to give whatever they could in support of the community center. This all happened within only two hours of my making the initial call to the radio station. I took a few moments to ponder the power of one small action taken to help others unconditionally.

The next day arrived, and this was the day for my final good deed, number five. I was wanting to tell someone about what I had been experiencing but knew that I couldn't. I purchased a copy of the *Boulder Daily News,* and on the front page was an article with the headline, "What If You Didn't Know Where

Your Next Meal Was Coming From?" It was a wonderful article. It addressed HIV and AIDS from the standpoint that it is everyone's problem and that the disease has touched almost all of our lives, whether we knew it or not. The article also featured a short interview with a woman who was married with two children. One of her children was infected with HIV. She had relied on the local food bank many times and urged others in the community to give. The article was written with such warmth and concern for those in need. It touched my soul.

After reading the article and reviewing my previous good deeds, I was at a loss to know what my fifth, and final, good deed would be. I was still amazed at the magnitude of giving that stemmed from one anonymous phone call and one fax. I thought about how different things would have been for me that day had I not made that call or sent the fax. I immediately felt an emptiness inside. I was also thankful to have met my friend Bill and knew that none of this would have happened had I not met him. The deeds that I had been performing made me feel enriched inside, even though I hadn't told anyone about them.

I didn't know what to do next and moved through my day at work in somewhat of a daze. Rod, the cute guy, had come into the club, and I didn't even notice him until he was leaving. I was alone at the front desk as Rod approached to leave. I retrieved his membership card and smiled while handing him his card. "Hey Rod."

He smiled as he took the card and placed it back in his wallet. "Thanks Don," Rod replied.

As he turned to leave, I wondered why he had called me Don. Then he turned back around, pointed at me, smiled and then laughed. "Gotch ya!"

I smiled back. We looked at each other for more than an extended moment. An arm touched my shoulder. I jumped and turned around. It was Keith.

"Jumpy, jumpy."

Keith startled me. Rod waved, then turned and made his way to the club exit as I watched.

"You two would make a cute couple," Keith said. I smiled in embarrassment. Keith patted my shoulder, turned, and walked away.

Something very disturbing happened that afternoon. I was in the locker room, taking a short break after a workout, when I overheard two people talking about the article in the paper regarding the community center.

"I think they should dig a big pit and throw all those faggots in it. If it wasn't for them, this whole AIDS thing never would have happened." These words were being spoken by a voice that was unfamiliar to me.

The comment shocked me and sent a jolt of fear throughout my entire body. My insecurities about being gay immediately resurfaced. I continued to dress, but was also curious as to who would have made these highly insensitive comments. I was about to walk out of the locker room when I noticed a member, Marty, a thirty-something male making a beeline in the direction the comment had come from.

"My brother was gay and died of AIDS you hateful asshole!" That's all he said; he then moved swiftly past me and out of the locker room, mumbling more obscenities under his breath.

As I made my way out of the locker room, from back in the corner, I heard the individual who had first spoken these hateful words. "How rude of him."

His comment created a surge of anger in me. I thought that if I had seen this man at that very moment, I might have done something that I would not only later regret but that would also cause me to lose my job at the club. I moved past a locker room mirror and noticed how red my face was. I then proceeded out of the locker room and treated myself to a cold drink of water from the adjacent drinking fountain. As I drank, the door to the locker room opened, and out walked Peter Riker, a very nice, middle-aged member. I looked directly at Peter.

"Hey Peter." Another man then came out of the locker room, one whom I did not recognize.

"Drew, I'd like you to meet my brother, Mark. He's visiting."

"Hello," Mark said.

The moment he spoke, I knew that his was the voice that had made those hateful comments. I did not extend my hand.

Peter looked at Mark. "Mark was just trying to start a boxing match in the locker room."

"Oh really?" I was playing stupid.

"Mark's out here on some business, might be moving here. I thought I'd show him the club."

"Great," I said, forcing a smile and then walked away.

A short time later, I was alone at the front desk, and a man rushed into the club. It was Mark, Peter's brother. He was in a panic.

"Hey, could you call someone or get someone who has some jumper cables? Pete took off, and this damn rental car won't start."

I didn't say anything for a moment.

Mark pleaded again after looking at his watch. "Please, I've got a plane to catch."

My deeply angered emotions were still flowing; yet I tried not to let it show. I had a set of jumper cables in my car. My first thoughts were of retaliation. *What can I do to get back at this evil man?* I then took a deep breath, and upon doing so, an unfamiliar voice from somewhere inside of me said, *"This is your good deed number five."*

I knew that this would definitely be the hardest one yet. I was to help this guy, this man so full of bigotry and hatred towards homosexuals, and not tell another living soul about it. I thought that if I didn't help him, I would be able to pass this story on, which a part of me relished.

"I'll help you," I said. I don't even know where those words came from. I went outside, where I recovered the jumper cables from my car and hooked them up to his battery. The rental car started immediately. Mark jumped out of his car after it started, pulled a twenty dollar bill out of his wallet, and offered it to me. I declined and then wished him a safe journey home.

I went back into the club. I was in shock. In my entire life, I had never come face-to-face with a person filled with so much hate towards a group of people. *Was the fear of meeting this type of person one of the reasons why I had never told anyone that I was gay?* I couldn't stand the thought of that type of hate being directed towards me. I had often struggled, and continued to struggle, to accept that part of myself. I also had some amusing thoughts about how clueless Mark had been to the fact that a "faggot" had just helped him move through his own personal crisis. I looked out the window from inside the club and waved to Mark as he drove past in a flurry. I then turned and moved back to the front counter, smiling, good deed number five complete. I immediately thought of Bill. I looked forward to talking with him when he got back in town.

Seven

A few days later, I was working the front desk at the club, updating some members' files, while trying to greet incoming members, when I heard a man clear his throat. I responded before looking up.

"I'm sorry ... " I looked up to see Bill standing there. "Hey." I smiled.

Bill returned the smile. "I'm here to take you to lunch."

"Cool," I said. Keith agreed to watch the front desk while I took my lunch break.

I had really been enjoying the deli at the health food store, and as I was telling Bill this, he proceeded to drive right past the place.

"Where are we going?" I asked.

"So, how are the good deeds progressing?" Bill asked, seeming to totally ignore my question.

"I'm finished." There was a copy of the *Boulder Daily News* on the seat between us featuring a follow-up article about the food bank. I picked up the paper, "I sure wish I could tell you about my experiences."

"Well, they wouldn't count then, would they?" Bill said with a smile.

I scanned the article and read about how the community center was receiving so many food and toiletry donations that they were having trouble storing the excess. I didn't finish reading the article but placed the paper back down on the seat between us.

"There's a paper bag full of food in the backseat," Bill said.

I reached to the back and grabbed the bag.

"My wife makes a very nice lunch," he said.

I opened the bag, which was bursting with food.

Bill spoke, as I pulled out two sandwiches, handing one to him. "I thought we'd just go for a drive."

Bill drove, and I ate, handing him parcels of food now and then. There was very little conversation while we ate. Bill finished his second sandwich, then said, "You seem happier."

"How can you tell?" I asked, around a mouthful of food.

"I have another assignment for you," he said, changing the subject again.

"You do?"

"What is it that you think you are here to do, Drew?"

I wasn't exactly sure Bill's reasoning behind his question. "You mean like at the health club?"

"No."

"Like on this planet?" I asked.

"Yes. Exactly."

"I don't know, I never much thought about it." I was familiar with "mission statements" from a business course I had taken in college but had never really written one regarding my purpose on Earth. I did know that I enjoyed the fitness industry. All of a sudden, I remembered back to when Bill spoke that day in our program planning class. He spoke about how we were here to be who we are, share that with others, follow our dreams, and love.

"Remember when I first spoke to your class?" he asked.

"I was just thinking about that."

"Drew, my mission here is 'to be, to dream, and to love.'" His was so very precise.

"I don't really know what mine is," I admitted.

"How did you feel after doing the good deeds?"

"Great."

"Do you think that there is something else going on here?"

This question caught me off guard and also frightened me.

"I don't understand," I said.

"Do you believe in God?"

I knew it. My first thought was, *Bill is a Bible thumper.* I had been raised Catholic and never really connected with the religion even though I had attended church services for years. I quit attending when I went to college, much to the upset of my family. I didn't share most organized religions' views on gays. I challenged Bill. "Are you a Bible thumper?"

Bill immediately burst into laughter. "No, I am not," he howled.

"Well then, why did you ask me if I believed in God?"

"It really isn't any of my business, but I believe that there is something bigger than us going on here. I believe that we all have a spiritual guide, an angel, a higher power, a master, whatever you choose to call it, operating in and around our lives. Something bigger than our finite human selves, of which, at our core, we are all a part."

I threw the question back at Bill. "Do *you* believe in God?"

"Yes and no. Let me explain. I believe that an all-loving power exists in the Universe, one that I am very much a part of. I believe we are all a part of this. I do not believe in the traditional, 'man upstairs' type of God. The type that is ready to strike us down at any given instant."

"Do you believe in good and evil, Bill?"

"I have a problem with that. I believe that things just are."

"What do you mean?"

"It is only my personal judgment that labels something as good or evil, and in the big picture, what I may judge as good, another may judge as bad or evil."

"What about AIDS?" I asked.

Bill glanced momentarily at me, continuing to drive. "You mean, do I think it is a curse on homosexuals?"

This is exactly what I had meant. Bill knew and continued with his answer. "No. I do not. It is a disease. And to address the whats and whys of how this disease ever happened—I do not know. I believe there is a divine plan, Drew. We are all here to fulfill our role in that plan. My job is to find out what my role is and to fulfill it to the best of my ability. When things happen in life that I want to judge as bad, I can only bless them and know that the Universe is unfolding as it should."

"I have a problem with that." I fidgeted in my seat. "I was raised to think that God was all powerful, untouchable—that he could take my life at any minute. I had a real problem when I figured out that I was gay. I thought it was wrong and that I would go to hell when I died because of it. I never felt that I chose it. It's just a part of who I am."

Bill pulled the car over to the side of the road. He looked at me for an extended moment. "Do you believe in God, Drew?"

I didn't know what to say, and I hesitated for a moment before responding. "I ... I want to."

Bill reached into the backseat and grabbed his briefcase. He opened it ever so carefully and then pulled out a plastic-covered piece of parchment paper. I had no clue what he was up to.

Bill handed me the plastic-covered paper. "Here, take this paper. It is a special piece of parchment paper that I purchased in Egypt. On this paper, I would like you to write all of the qualities that a God of your choice would possess. I want you to create, in writing, your own concept of God. You don't even have to call it God; it can be a him, her, spiritual guide, master, anything. This is for only you. You don't have to share it with me or with anyone else when you are finished. But I would like to know when you have completed the work, that's all."

I took the paper graciously, thinking that this would be an interesting assignment. But I had another question for Bill. "You said that we all have a guide or master or whatever in our lives. How do you know when they are speaking, or which one to listen to?"

"I think that you are asking why I don't believe in just one source, one God? I do, Drew. The guides, masters, angels, or 'whatevers' are all part of the one God of my understanding. Basically, it's all love."

I was confused; I felt good, but confused. Bill started the car and pulled back onto the road and headed back towards Boulder. He gave me a wink. "Just try it."

I said I would. We drove back to the club. I jumped out of the car, carrying my special paper. Keith and Donna were waiting patiently to go to lunch. I waved to Bill as he drove off, and Keith came over to me.

"Hey, was that your new boyfriend?"

I wrinkled my forehead.

Keith laughed. "Just joking. That's Bill, right?"

I nodded.

"He's cool; kicked my ass at racquetball a few times."

Keith and Donna took off for lunch, and I went back into the health club. I placed the special paper behind the front desk. I wanted the afternoon to pass by quickly so that I could get home and work on the assignment. I was slightly fearful. I never knew I could formulate my own concept of God.

When Keith and Donna got back to the club, Keith asked if I would like to go out with a group of them from the club that night. I declined, and his next comment irritated me slightly. "You sure like to be alone a lot."

I wondered why the comment had bothered me. I didn't like to go out and party and hated to see people drunk and abusing their bodies. I was also feeling at the time much like what I imagined a caterpillar feels like when it's in a cocoon. I was going through some changes, some that I didn't understand and couldn't explain—but changes that I wanted to continue. I felt extremely vulnerable. I knew that in the past I avoided people and social gatherings because I didn't want people to find out that I was gay, but I had come to peace with the fact that this wasn't the current situation.

That evening, I sat in my apartment alone, a candle lit on the table. I had a nice pen and the clean piece of parchment paper that Bill had given me. I stared at the blank paper for quite some time. An hour passed and still the paper was blank. I didn't want to write the word God on the paper. I think this was out of fear, fear of the God I had been taught to believe in. I knew that concept of God didn't work for me any longer. I put the initials M.G. on top of the paper. M.G. stood for "My God" or "My Guide." I didn't have to explain this to anyone but myself and liked the idea that I could give those initials dual meaning. I then began to list all of the qualities that My Guide or My God would possess.

M.G.

All-Loving
All-Accepting
Powerful
Wise
Nonjudgmental
Kind
Easy to Talk to
A Best Friend

The short list took me until six the next morning. It was amazing that it took so long to come up with so few words. I was happy with my work. Although I had no physical image of what My Guide or God looked like, I at least had the descriptive words down on paper. I knew that any image of a guy in sandals and a beard was out. My immediate thought was to go to Bill's office, wait for him to show up, and share the work that I had completed with him, but it was still early. I decided to go for a run.

Eight

I'm not sure why I ventured into unknown territory that morning, but it was summer, and the nice, warm weather encouraged exploration. I ran on a new trail near the open space area close to where I lived. The trail was about a year old. I was about three miles into my run, when I noticed a man seated on a bench near a small stream that paralleled the new trail. The man was dressed in comfortable clothes and appeared to be asleep. I approached and slowed to a walk, focusing on the man. It was Bill. I wondered why he wasn't moving, and his lack of movement frightened me. I stepped in front of Bill. I couldn't tell if he was breathing or not. His eyes were closed, and I quietly said his name. "Bill?"

He did not respond, and I became concerned. I slowly reached out to touch his arm. It was cold. I took a deep breath, and just as I looked at his eyes, they opened. He then let out a deep breath. I jumped back, holding my breath. A moment passed, and then, as if on cue, we both burst into laughter.

"I thought you were dead!"

"I was." Bill continued to laugh, but I immediately stopped. I didn't understand the joke. Bill stretched his arms and then stood up, "I was dead to the world. I was meditating," he explained.

"Oh."

Bill put one of his legs perpendicular on the bench and stretched. "You must have finished your assignment?"

"I have. How did you know?"

Bill lowered the leg and raised the other to stretch. "We wouldn't have run into each other if you hadn't." Bill lowered his leg and looked at me. "Drew, have you ever used visualization for sports, before a meet, or for your training?"

"Sure. For swimming, our coach would have us close our eyes, and he would have us visualize an event, sometimes an entire swim meet, every event. Mental training, he called it. He would even use a stopwatch sometimes."

"Mental training is a form of meditation. When I meditate to get in touch with My Guide or My God, I just close my eyes, let the thoughts of the day come and go until it is silent. That is when the still, quiet voice of God can speak to me."

I was slightly confused but very interested after hearing Bill speak of "God and Guide." The same two words that I had come up with.

"I think I understand."

"Your coach was leading you through a meditation. How did you do in those events?"

"We went to state that year and really kicked ass!"

"So it worked then?"

"Yeah. Sure, I guess."

"Well, Drew, when we meditate, we first close our eyes and focus on our breathing. Then the mind usually begins to race. Thoughts about what productive things we should be doing, bills that are unpaid, work schedules, on and on. In meditation, we do not judge these thoughts; we let them come and let them go. Finally our mind will clear. It is then that we can invite our God or our Guide into our lives so that we may be led on our journey here."

At that moment, I felt that I truly believed what Bill was saying.

"How do you do that?"

"That's why I had you do the last assignment. If you have a concept of a loving God or Guide in your life, even if you don't have an image, the words can help. Ultimately, it is love that you are opening up to allow in."

I was enjoying listening to him.

"Have you ever been thinking of someone and they happen to call you on the phone?"

I nodded in affirmation.

"This is your God energy or love, tapped into that of another. These are things *we* call coincidences. The Universe calls it 'synchronicity.'"

I blurted out, "Like what keeps happening to you and me? How we keep running into each other?"

"Exactly. The Universe is always leading us in the direction of spiritual growth, towards love. But much of the time we are too busy or afraid or numb and we stray."

I heard and felt the truth in what it was that Bill was saying.

"Drew, I would like you to try to meditate, starting tomorrow. First, read over what you have written on the paper and then lovingly invite that definition to join you in your meditation."

I was frightened again for some reason. This was all so new to me.

"Anything new can be frightening. Remember the swim meets."

This put me instantly at ease. I had practiced a form of meditation; this would just be taking it a step further.

Bill patted me on the shoulder, "It may be difficult at first but stick with it—I'm leaving town for a month."

"A month?" I said.

"I'm going on an extended speaking engagement: London, Germany, and France. I'd like you to set aside thirty minutes a day for the next month to meditate. You can put on some soft music at home and sit quietly, or come here. I would also like you to buy a notebook. Write down the words you choose to describe your Guide or God in the notebook and then write down what happens after you meditate."

"Why write it down?"

"It will make sense to you as time progresses. I'll see you when I get back."

He gave me a hug; I hugged him back. I felt such a genuine sense of unconditional love coming from this man. Bill then turned and walked away, down the path. I watched as he moved out of sight.

I looked at my watch. It was 7 a.m. This was my day off, and I didn't usually start at the health club until 9 a.m. Our swim coach used to really stress the importance of discipline. He said it was easier to train yourself if you trained at the same time every day. I believed this, and so I decided that I would try to meditate at 7 a.m. every day. I took a seat on the same bench that Bill had just occupied.

I closed my eyes and tried to think about what I had written on the parchment paper. The only words I could remember were *all-loving.* Next, I inhaled and exhaled a few times and then it happened. My mind starting racing like an engine. *You need to do laundry. This is stupid. Faggot. Do something constructive. Why don't you go into work today? I forgot to mail the phone bill.* This continued for the entire half hour. I thought I was going crazy. I almost couldn't stand it, but I forced myself to sit there, through all of the chatter. I opened my eyes a few times while I was seated there. I would hear someone move past or a branch rustle. A bird started chirping and wouldn't stop, and that bothered me. I was extremely relieved when the half hour ended.

My first attempt at meditation was unsuccessful, and I was glad that it was over. I knew that it wouldn't be easy and it surely wasn't.

I ran home, and on the way, a thought entered my mind. *"Every journey begins with the first step."*

I had no idea where the thought had come from. Then I remembered my high school swim coach telling us how lucky we were to have all of the different sports that we did at our school to choose from. He told us if we tried one, even for only a short time, we'd probably have some idea if we were going to like it or not. He also said that if we never tried anything we'd never know. I never thought that I would like the swim team and getting up at five in the morning for practice. I didn't like getting up early for the first couple of weeks, but I loved to swim. After about a month, I began to look forward to getting up and swimming. I came to believe that it was a great way to start the day. I carried that experience with me and almost always exercised first thing in the morning. I thought about all of this as I ran home.

I stopped by the neighborhood grocery store and bought a notebook to write in as Bill had suggested. Upon entering my apartment, I made my way to a small desk in my room. I sat down, opened the notebook, and, referring to the beautiful parchment paper, wrote the words that described My Guide followed by, "Meditation. Day One. 'Hard'."

I spent the rest of that day with a college buddy, Kyle, who called out of the blue. Kyle was visiting Boulder after having moved away to Seattle for a job.

We hung out and talked about what each of us had been doing since college. It was pleasant. He was leaving that night but had wanted to reconnect with a few friends. Kyle told me that he had started journaling lately. I thought the timing of his comment odd, due to the fact that I had just made my first journal entry that day in the notebook I bought. We spent a short time together, and then off he went.

The entire first week of practice with meditation was much the same. I would get up, go for a short run, and then make my way to the bench where I had first discovered Bill meditating. I would then sit and read through what I had written about my new concept of God: all-loving, all-accepting, powerful, wise, nonjudgmental, kind, easy to talk to, a best friend. I would then close my eyes, concentrate on my breathing, and then, for thirty minutes, my mind would unleash an array of chatter, running wild in my head, much to my extreme discomfort. These were the longest half hours of the day. I fought sitting there and listening to the busyness of my mind. One day, it took all of the discipline I had in my entire system to keep from getting up. Many times, I thought I was going crazy just listening to my own thoughts. *When would the chatter end?*

It was the third day of the second week that I

noticed a slight change during my meditation practice. I would drift off for a short time during the thirty minutes. Where? I was unsure. But afterwards, I thought the short amount of time that I was unable to account for during the meditation was a good sign. I was making some progress and proud of myself for sticking with it. I thought a lot about my swim coach and my previous experiences with him. The discipline had prepared me to go through with this difficult assignment. I wrote about all of this in my notebook.

The first day of the third week, I began to notice that the busy thoughts that had previously rushed through my head during meditation had eased. I was losing track of more and more time during the thirty minutes. I was also feeling much more relaxed afterwards. A number of people at work pointed this out to me; and they all said that I seemed so content and mellow. I told Janet, the owner of the club, that I had started meditating.

"It figures," she said, alluding to a favorite pastime of Boulder residents.

It was hard for me to explain, at that point, what meditation really was doing for me. I don't think that I was having any major revelations during the reflective time. I was just excited to continue with the assignment.

One Wednesday evening, I arrived home to a message from Mary, Bill's secretary. She said that Bill had checked in with her and asked her to call and inform me that Bill had forgotten to tell me about a weekly meditation group at the spiritual center in downtown Boulder. They met on Wednesday nights. This was great, I thought—a room full of people with scattered thoughts going through their minds all together in one place! I called the center and got some information. The meditation lasted for one hour and the format was that of a guided meditation. I didn't know what to expect but decided to attend that evening.

I arrived at the spiritual center that night. It was a very plain building, inside and out. I discovered the meditation room. It was dimly lit with nearly one hundred candles; soft Native American music played a soothing chant. There were people seated on the floor and in folding chairs. Others were simply lying on the floor. I felt a sense of peace when I entered the room. I took a seat in the first available folding chair. I looked around the room. It seemed to me that everyone was already meditating—their eyes were closed and no one was talking. I looked at my watch; it was only five minutes until seven. I had been told that the meditation didn't begin until seven. Maybe I was late.

There was a small stack of pillows up in the front of the room on an elevated portion of the floor. It looked like an altar of some sort. Candles surrounded the pillows. I turned around to scan the people seated in the back of the room. I did a double take. There was Rod, the cute guy from the club. His eyes were closed. I also noticed that there were all different types of people in the room, a diverse slice of life.

I turned back to face the front of the room as a woman made her way to the small altar and positioned herself comfortably atop the pillows. She then closed her eyes and took a few deep breaths. I think at that point I was the only one in the room with their eyes open. I guessed that this was the beginning of the meditation so I closed my eyes. My mind took off once again. *I wonder if anyone is staring at me? What are all of these people doing here? Is this a cult? Is Rod gay? Maybe he's here with a girlfriend. What is meditation?*

As if on cue, the woman in the front of the room began to speak. "What is meditation? Meditation is an opportunity for us to quiet our minds. A time for us to connect to our spiritual center, an opportunity for us to listen to our inner guides and masters. So, let us do that now."

An answer to my unspoken question. I popped open my eyes and quickly looked around the room again, then turned back, closing my eyes.

The woman continued. "We will begin by taking three deep breaths."

I opened my eyes again. I just wanted to see what was going on. Everyone's eyes were still closed. I closed my eyes once again and joined in on the second inhale and exhale.

"And inhale, ... and exhale."

A number of silent moments passed after the breathing until she spoke again.

"Now I ask that you open your hearts. Let the thoughts of the day flow in and flow out. Good. Just concentrate on your breathing. Good. Let us now take this time to ask our Guide, God, or Spirit to be with us. Let us take this time to allow our finite human selves to let us know God, to know love, to know light." She didn't say anything more for a time. The music continued to play, and I finally began to relax. I drifted off.

I was in some sort of cave. It was dark. A short way off in the distance there was this beautiful defined light. I believe that it was indigo in color. The color was so very crisp. I was headed towards the direction of the light, when I heard the woman's voice again.

" ... to know love, to know light. Slowly coming back to the room. Feel your body connecting with the floor or the chair."

I immediately felt the chair beneath me and had lost all sight of the light in the cave. I opened my eyes. Most everyone else in the room still had their eyes closed. I looked at my watch. It was eight o'clock. I couldn't believe it! An entire hour had passed as if it had only been minutes. This amazed me.

The woman spoke for a short time after the meditation. I have no clue what she said. I wanted to know more about where I had gone during the meditation. *Where was that cave? And that light? It was so beautiful. Did this really happen? Maybe I was losing my mind?* I do know that I remember incense was burning in the room.

One last thing the woman said was that there was herbal tea ready if anyone wished to stay.

"Bless you all, and good night," she finally said.

I did not stay to have tea. I moved with a small crowd towards the door. Outside, I noticed Rod walking towards his car. I don't know if he saw me or not. I made my way to my car and got in. I was feeling quite euphoric. I drove home enveloped by an extreme feeling of peace.

I had the deepest sleep that night. I don't know if I dreamed or not, but the next morning I awoke feeling so alive and calm. I was excited to take my morning run and then to meditate. I wanted to have the cave and that beautiful light appear once again in my meditation. I arrived at the bench on the trail. I went through my personal ritual: reading the definition of My Guide, breathing, then closing my eyes. I hoped that I would be able to go back to the beautiful place that I had visited the previous evening. All that happened was a bird chirping overhead for thirty minutes. I was discouraged and felt that my breakthrough of the night before had been almost nonexistent. I did hold out, though, for the entire thirty minutes and was proud of myself for doing so. I then ran back home, still slightly frustrated, and I readied myself for work.

Nine

I was slightly out of it at work that day. Janet said hello to me five times before I acknowledged her. My mind was focused on the light that I had seen in the cave, the beautiful, crisp, indigo light.

Later on that morning, I was finishing a tour of the club with a few potential members when I noticed Rod working out in the weight room. I finished the tour and made my way to the weight room. I felt driven to connect with Rod after seeing him at meditation. I intercepted Rod at the weight-room drinking fountain.

"Hey Rod." Rod looked up to me after drinking some water. His blue eyes pierced my soul. Rod raised his eyebrows to me in acknowledgment, and we stared at each other for a moment.

"Man, you have great eyes." I couldn't believe the words that had just come out of my mouth. After I realized what I had said, I immediately became embarrassed.

"Thank you," he said.

I had wanted to tell him that I had seen him the previous night but that certainly wasn't what came out of my mouth. I didn't know what to do next, so I turned and walked away. I looked back for a second when I reached the weight room door. Rod was still staring at me and smiling. Overwhelmed, I left the weight room. I felt as if I was on a cloud the remainder of the day.

The following day, the sun made its presentation through a small group of clouds, creating one of the most incredible sunrises I've ever witnessed. I took a longer run than usual and then made my way to the familiar bench to meditate. I went through my meditation ritual and then sat there with my eyes closed. I felt extremely relaxed.

I was instantly back in the cave. I moved towards the beautiful, crisp, indigo light. The cave was dark, but the light was inviting to me, calling me to move towards it. There was a feeling of peace in this place. I moved closer to the sharp light. I felt so serene, being in this place. I felt as if my being was now intertwined with a divine presence. A figure approached from behind the light. It appeared to be male, but it was transparent. There was an angelic presence about this being. I wondered who or what this presence was.

I opened my eyes as I heard footsteps behind me on the path. I quickly turned to witness a runner out for a morning jaunt. I looked to my watch; it had been exactly thirty minutes.

These meditation experiences were amazing to me. I sat and pondered things for a short time. I realized that for the first time in my life I was interested in something other than sports and work. It was as if I had embarked on a wonderful new journey into the nature of my existence. I was excited to discover more. I wanted to know who the being was that had appeared behind that light in my meditation. Again, I wrote all of this down in my notebook.

I enjoyed my job, but thoughts about what was to happen with it or my career now or in the future weren't of great importance to me. This was a new type of thinking for me. I was raised to believe that in order to experience life you had to work hard and set material goals, and that would create happiness.

I thought about my family and wondered if anyone in my immediate family was truly happy. I couldn't answer this. I know the peace and tranquility that I had been experiencing since my introduction to Bill was unlike any other experience in my life up to that point. It was all derived from nothing directly outside of my own being. I thought about the good deeds exercise and how by not telling anyone about them gave me so much pleasure inside. It was a feeling of unconditional love towards others reflecting back into my soul.

I was excited for the next Wednesday night to arrive so that I could attend the group meditation once again. I was also looking forward to seeing Bill so that I could tell him about all of the wondrous experiences that I had discovered thus far during my meditations.

People continued to notice changes in me at work. I noticed that certain things that used to bother me didn't seem to any longer. A few people who worked at the front desk had the habit of using various front desk items and not putting them back where they found them. We had a proper place for everything—be it a stapler, towels, pencils, membership cards, or anything else. They seemed to find new homes constantly. This used to frustrate and irritate me, and I found that it no longer did. I also began to entertain the thought of participating in some type of volunteer work.

I remember my father telling me when I was young that, "Unless you're getting paid for it, it isn't worth doing." I was now learning the exact opposite was true. I know that at first, I wanted to bust out of college, make money, climb the corporate ladder in the fitness industry, and open my own health club. My thoughts and feelings around these goals were now being challenged.

The following Tuesday, I went for my morning run and took my place upon the bench where I had been meditating for almost an entire month now. I went through my ritual as usual, and then a question rushed into my mind. *Who is the individual in the cave?* I proceeded to meditate.

I was instantly back in the cave. I moved slowly towards the indigo light, this time noticing the smells and the hollow sounds of this natural carving. I noticed that the indigo light was coming from atop what appeared to be an altar-like formation of rocks. I could taste the magical moisture in the cave. It had a tint of honey to it. I moved closer to the altar and then rested there with my eyes fixed on the beautiful light. I felt a warmth inside my body, and then, I looked up to see the being standing there to greet me again. It was definitely transparent. Feelings of warmth and peace intensified inside of my body in its presence. I didn't know what was happening. I smiled at the being. I felt that it wanted to communicate with me. This being was My Guide. I then asked a question of the being.

"Are you God?" Once again, I felt an intensity of emotion rush through my body, and the answer came to me, as if through my entire body. A peaceful, still voice answered. "We are all parts of the greater whole—God, as you may."

I didn't know what the words meant but my heart understood. I didn't know what else to ask. I just stood there smiling at this presence, feeling a serene inner warmth.

After a short time, I opened my eyes and became aware of my surroundings as I sat on the bench in the open space area. I sat for a moment. I thought that I should have asked the being what its name was and why I couldn't see it. I had never felt at such peace with anyone or anything in my entire life up until that point. It was strange. The closest I had actually ever felt to that feeling I was having was when I was in Bill's presence, and it was nothing sexual. It was a feeling of total peace, love, and acceptance, far beyond words.

The following day was Wednesday. I decided not to meditate after my run in the morning, since I would be going to the group meditation that evening. I wondered, *Could you meditate too much?* I noticed that my day didn't seem to flow as well as the previous days had when I meditated in the morning.

Rod was at the club that day. I told him that I had seen him at meditation the week before. He told me that he had been attending the weekly sessions for about a year. Somehow I got up the nerve to ask him if he would be going to meditation that night. He told me that his parents were visiting, and he had decided to spend some time with them and wouldn't be going. He said he hadn't seen them in years. Rod seemed distraught when he spoke of his family. I wondered why he hadn't seen his parents in such a long time, but didn't ask. I decided I would still attend the group meditation that night.

I arrived at the spiritual center about fifteen minutes early and noticed that there were quite a few people there already. I was not as nervous this time since I knew more of what to expect. I also began to think about life and how so many people miss out on so much because of fear—fear of trying something new, fear of taking the first step, or fear of doing something alone.

At promptly seven o'clock, the same woman from the previous week took her place on the pillows surrounded by an angelic illumination of candles. I had trouble keeping my eyes closed. Again, I kept wondering if people were staring at me. Once she started to speak, I felt more at ease.

"Welcome."

I closed my eyes.

"We will begin the meditation this evening with a focus upon our breathing. Please join me in taking three deep breaths."

We all inhaled and exhaled three times together.

"God's energy is in all of us. We are all a part of the light. Wherever we are, the light is always there with us."

I do not know if she spoke anymore.

I was immediately back into the cave, moving again towards the crisp and clear illumination resting upon the altar of rocks. All of my senses were highly active. I could smell the warmth of the honey moisture in the air. My hearing was at its peak. I felt as if I was pure emotion and senses, aware of everything. My Guide greeted me at the altar of light. I noticed that the figure was still blurry. I could see right through it. At this point, I wasn't sure if it was male or female; I just took in the beauty of its transparent form. I was not afraid.

My Guide then spoke to me again, "You wish to know me and my purpose?"

These were my exact thoughts without verbalizing them. I acknowledged the question.

"I am here as a Guide to you. I have been with you all along your journey, first unconsciously and now in your consciousness, in your conscious God mind." The communication continued, "You have much to ask of me, but I must first lay the groundwork for you."

I remained open to receive what it was that was being communicated to me.

"As your Guide, I am a connection to the light of which you are a vital part. The light of which we are all a part. Every single individual on this Earth is a piece of the light. This light's source is love. We are all of this, and it is of God. You must understand this from the very beginning. We all have a Guide to call upon, some more than one. Many people are out of touch with their Guide and their connection to the light, and thus they exist in the darkness. Many are caught up in the physical illusion and thus do not connect with the light. We are called many things, but in the end, we are all of God. And God is love. This is the bottom line of understanding.

"I speak the truth that you seek. It is your truth. Others may disagree with you, and that is their choice. Others may also agree with you and that is their choice, as well.

"Each and every person on this Earth plane is here to experience spiritual growth. Live your truth and do not press it upon others. You may share your beliefs as part of who you are, but let others have theirs, too.

"One of our ultimate lessons here is to follow our own path and to bless others as they make their journey through their lifetime. Remain true to yourself and know that when others challenge you in your beliefs, it is only an opportunity to strengthen your own inner beliefs. Some may offer harsh criticism of you and your beliefs. Remember this is only their fear speaking. Center yourself and offer them love as best as you are able.

"Know that nothing that comes from love can ever fail. And remember that you are from love. What it is that you do with the love available to you and the God-given gifts bestowed upon you, is ultimately up to you. You ***do*** *have free will. Use all of your gifts wisely. This is the information offered to you. You are blessed and loved."*

"Now feel the chair or the floor beneath you and slowly bring your presence back to the room."

I felt the chair under me and then opened my eyes. It took me a few moments to bring my eyes back into focus. I felt as if I had traveled somewhere. It took me awhile to adjust to being back in the room. After about five minutes, I felt that I was able to stand. I believe that I was one of the last to leave the building. I walked slowly back to my car, trying to remember all that had happened. I was given so much information.

Who was My Guide? Why couldn't I see the figure completely and clearly?

I had many questions. I was also frightened again. However, I knew deep in my heart, that everything that was happening to me was a necessary part of my continuing journey this lifetime. I knew that I was exactly where I was supposed to be at this time in the Universe, no matter how strange I was feeling. The changes and experiences seemed to be happening to me so quickly.

I arrived home. I then just sat and wrote in my notebook for a short while. I tried to remember what wisdom My Guide had shared with me. I thought of him as male yet he seemed almost sexless. In his presence, I felt pure love. I didn't want to tell anyone about my experience except for Bill. Anyone else might think I was crazy. I felt comfortable discussing these things with Bill and really no one else at this time. I trusted Bill and never felt any judgment from him. I also knew that whatever I told him would be received with unconditional love. This had been proven to me when I shared with him that I was gay. I felt the urge to call Bill, but it was late.

The next day I did call Bill's office. Mary answered the phone and told me that Bill was not due back for another couple of days. Mary told me that Bill had told her when they last spoke that he sensed I was making some major progress in my spiritual growth. I assured her that his senses were correct. I really wanted to get together with Bill that day. I did not have to work and had no other plans. I had already meditated with some difficulty that morning. I think I was overwhelmed by the information presented to me by My Guide the previous night.

I began to have thoughts about what to do with my day. *I could get a massage.* The massage therapist at the club had offered me one. I really didn't want to go into the club on my day off. *I could go on a hike. I could go shopping.* I didn't really like to shop. *Maybe I would call Rod and ask if he would like to do something.* My mind was very busy. With all of these thoughts spinning in my head, I decided to try to meditate once again.

I put a CD in my stereo. The soothing music calmed my racing mind. I closed my eyes and then took a number of deep breaths.

I was back inside of the cave. It was more vivid than I had experienced before. I moved towards the beautiful indigo light. I now felt extremely calm. I felt a feeling of warmth and love overcome my entire being.

My Guide then appeared behind the light; unrecognizable once again. The communication commenced as his image quietly spoke to me.

"The human experience is one of greatness. We busy ourselves in order to avoid getting to know the true self—ours and others. We are no more than spirits having experiences in the human form. It is interesting how we make the attempt to keep ourselves separate from each other, creating distances between human forms through races, cultures, subcultures, separately held beliefs, and even sexualities.

"Drew, part of your journey is to seek out what it is that you are here to do. Ultimately, we are all here to do nothing more than to just be. And at the core, this is love. We are all unique expressions of love. When we realize that we are all true expressions of love, we can then choose the unique ways in which we will express that love. Many call this 'living the dream.' Through our acceptance and expressions of ourselves as love, we advance spiritually. The key to this is to remember who we are and to live that each moment of our existence.

The physical allows us to experience this love and grow within it in every experience that we encounter. Some call these 'life lessons.' And it is often through what we perceive as the most difficult 'life lessons' and experiences that we are offered the most opportunity to grow into love. This is why we have bodies. Our spirits need to have mobility in this human form.

"Trust inside in the direction you are to move this day as in everyday. Be in the moment and listen to your inner guidance. With practice, you will know and choose the correct direction in life. You may stray at times, as all do, but the path will be presented to you once again. The human condition offers free will. 'Be still and know.'" My Guide then concluded. "I love you and care for you."

The image then disappeared, and the indigo light remained. I stood still, looking into the light and feeling so very enlightened after having been given many loving messages about life. It was as if I had spoken to God directly. I felt as if I had been blanketed in total love. But I wanted to know the face of My Guide. Why wouldn't the image come into focus?

I opened my eyes just as the music was finishing. I looked at the clock. It had been exactly thirty minutes.

I sat for a short time and reviewed what had just happened in this meditation. I then arose and made my way to the kitchen and poured myself a glass of water. It was strange, but as I drank the water, I felt it pass through my entire body with ease, cleansing me. The comment from the meditation about being in the moment and being myself came to me. I then began to think about being gay. I wondered why it was that I was so afraid to let people know about this part of who I was. I briefly entertained the idea of telling everyone at the club. I then imagined everyone accepting it totally. The next thing I thought of was the locker room incident and Peter Riker's brother. This frightened me. I knew there have been people killed for being and expressing who they were. I had many more questions.

I mentally listed the questions that I had. *Why, if we are all here as expressions of love, do we harm each other? Why are there wars? Why do people kill? Why are people gay?* A thought then instantly entered my mind.

"We are all unique expressions of love."

Maybe I had retained more of the meditation than I had thought. This put me at ease. I wanted so much to reconnect with Bill. I needed to talk to someone about the questions and thoughts I was having. An unrelated thought then entered my mind.

"Go to the the gay community center today and ask them how you may be of service."

I retracted, and another thought followed.

"Sometimes we resist the very thing that we are to do."

Where were these thoughts coming from?

I wasn't meditating any longer, and yet, someone or something was speaking to me. I wondered if it was possible to meditate while my eyes were open. I thought about what had been said to me and then decided to follow the words that had been delivered. Maybe my reaction was only a form of fear. I set the fear aside and made my way to the door.

Ten

As I opened the door to the gay community center, I was immediately greeted by a friendly, thin woman, probably in her forties. She was seated behind the front desk and appeared a bit frazzled.

She smiled at me. "Hello, may I help you with something?"

"Yeah, I just thought I would stop in here today and see if you needed help with anything."

She looked up towards the skylight above her and spoke. "Thank you."

I wasn't sure who she was thanking at that immediate moment but later understood. She arose and moved out from behind the desk to greet me.

"I'm Barbara Whitman, the volunteer coordinator

here at the community center. Everyone calls me Barb."

"Drew, Drew Wilson."

"I had two volunteers cancel on me today. So, I'm trying to coordinate things and answer the phone along with eight hundred other things! We have a mailing that must go out today, and I have only one person here to help stuff the envelopes. I would be so grateful if you would be willing to help him."

"Sure," I answered, without hesitation.

Barb took my hand and led me into the next room where Rod stood, stuffing envelopes. My jaw almost hit the floor.

Barb began to speak as Rod turned around. "Rod, this is Drew."

"We know each other. Hey," Rod smiled and stuck his hand out. We shook.

"Great, I'm sure you two can handle this little project then."

"No problem," Rod answered.

The telephone rang, and Barb disappeared out the door and back into the reception area.

Rod and I stood there for a moment, looking at each other. He broke the ice, picking up a flyer, explaining the envelope-stuffing process, "It's pretty easy, you just take the folded flyer and stick it in the envelope, then seal it with this sponge dabber." Rod completed stuffing and sealing an envelope. I moved near the table and positioned myself in front of a stack of envelopes and flyers and started to stuff the envelopes. We were both silent for a short period of time.

After a very short while, I spoke. "How long have you been volunteering here?"

"Well, about a year. I usually answer the phones on Saturdays, but Barb called me today because she was in a major bind."

There was silence again. I was so excited that Rod was here but tried to remain cool to that fact. I now definitely knew that I had been led to the right place this day and blessed that unknown voice for suggesting that I come to the community center.

We continued to stuff envelopes, and our conversation grew. There isn't much brain power required to stuff envelopes.

Rod was the first to pop the question. "So, are you gay?"

I was surprised at his bluntness but felt no threat in answering. I looked directly at him.

"Yes, I am."

"I thought so, but I wasn't quite sure."

"Are you?" I asked back.

Rod grabbed another envelope and answered while stuffing a flyer inside. "Since the day I was born."

"Do you think people are born gay?" I asked.

"I know that I was. For as long as I can remember, I have been attracted to men. I've always enjoyed women, but there was something missing when I was with a woman. With men, I seem to be more emotionally, spiritually, and physically connected. And I like that; the relationships are much more fulfilling for me."

I could relate to every word coming out of Rod's mouth. "I've always wondered if I turned out to be gay because my father was so strict or maybe because he traveled a lot on business when I was little."

Rod smiled at me.

"I had girlfriends in high school and in college," I continued.

"So, when did you know that you were gay?" Rod asked.

I picked up a stack of stuffed envelopes and placed them into an empty box. "I guess a part of me has always known. I think I dated girls because that was what society told me was 'right.' I have two older brothers. They would always tell me about their escapades with women, usually telling me much more than I was interested in hearing."

"Was your father gone a lot when your brothers were growing up?"

I didn't understand what he was getting at. "Huh?"

"You said that you thought you might have turned out gay because your father was absent, so shouldn't your brothers be gay then, too?"

"Thanks." I got the point Rod was trying to make.

"I tried to be straight for years," he said.

"Me too. I would go out with girls and do the very things that my brothers had told me that they did with women sexually, and I just didn't get anything out of it. I thought that there was something wrong with me." Rod nodded his head in agreement, as I continued. "I had a girlfriend in college. I loved everything about her, but something was missing.

"One day, I was in the library, studying. I looked up from my books and this attractive guy was staring at me. I looked away and then looked back, and he was still staring at me. I looked down at my books for a few moments and then back up again, and he was *still* staring. I felt uncomfortable and yet excited at the same time. Nothing ever happened between us. He never came over and introduced himself, and I eventually left the library. I never saw him again.

"That night, I was with my girlfriend, and all I could think about was the guy from the library. It really frightened me. Not the fact that I was gay but that I was living a lie. I wasn't being fair to my girlfriend or to myself. We had talked one time about how awful it would be to be married, have children, and then find out that your spouse was gay. It would be devastating."

"It happens a lot," said Rod.

"I broke up with my girlfriend. It was a pretty messy thing," I responded, in a reflective tone.

Rod moved a bunch of envelopes that we had both been stuffing and placed them in an empty box on the floor.

"So, have you ever had sex with a woman?"

I was slightly embarrassed. "Well, with my girlfriend, we were going to one night—in my brother's apartment, while he and his girlfriend were out for dinner. We tried, but I just couldn't perform sexually. I enjoyed holding her, but for some reason, I just couldn't get excited. I really thought that there was something very wrong with me. I mean I was nineteen, at my sexual prime, and ... nothing."

Rod moved next to me and placed his hand on my shoulder. "There's nothing wrong with you."

I fought back a tear. "Have you ever?"

"Never. Never even tried, but I sure used to lie about it." His mood seemed to change. I didn't pry. There was an extended silence in the room.

I felt that we both wanted to know more about each other. I was really enjoying the conversation with Rod. I lightened things up with my next question. "What do you do for a living?" Rod handed me some more flyers, as my stack was running low.

"I'm a sports marketer. I 'rep' a few new sports products. I travel, but I'm my own boss pretty much, and I really enjoy that."

I thought that was very cool. Whatever Rod did for a living didn't really much matter to me. I was just enjoying getting to know him. I had wanted this moment to occur, and it did, without any help from me. It was as if the Universe had just allowed it.

Rod asked me another question. "So, where do you see yourself going with your work at the health club?"

"I've always wanted to own my own health club, and they offered me a job after I graduated, so I took it."

"You didn't answer my question."

He was right. "I don't know exactly. I think things are turning out a little different than what I had expected."

"What do you mean?"

I didn't really want to get into it at this point, so I changed the subject. "I don't really want to get into it right now—do you always work out alone?"

Rod didn't push the topic any further. "Cool. I really like the club. I like to lift weights by myself. I kinda get into a zone when I'm lifting. It helps me to get through the workout."

"I hear ya."

"I think some of the people at the club just think I'm stuck up. I'm not; I just like to work out alone. I've also had a few of the female members try to hit on me. I'm not always open about my sexual orientation in the sports world."

I was relating one hundred percent to what Rod was saying. "I think who people sleep with doesn't have to be such a public thing," I said.

"Isn't it funny how so many heterosexuals love to tell you all about who they're having sex with, and then when the topic of homosexuality comes up, they don't want to hear anything about it?"

I nodded in agreement, and Rod continued. "When will people figure out that love is love and it's not about the sex?"

The question needed no explanation or further comment. We looked at each other and smiled.

Rod and I took a break from the mundane task of stuffing envelopes. Barb popped in and said that it was break time and then offered to pay for our lunch. We declined with grace and decided to walk to a nearby restaurant.

As we walked to the restaurant, Rod told me that Barb had had an eighteen-year-old son who died of AIDS about five years ago. After that, she started to do volunteer work at the community center. Then, about a year ago, the volunteer coordinator position opened up, and she got it. She didn't have a lot of money, but she had a heart worth millions. I was so thankful, once again, that I had gotten the inner message to make my way to the community center that day.

Eleven

We ate lunch at The Sage, a very healthy Boulder restaurant. Our conversation continued as we ate. Rod told me that when he first informed his parents that he was gay, they kicked him out of the house. He was only fifteen. He stayed with a friend for almost a year and then moved back home. He lied to his parents, and told them that he had been wrong about his sexuality. Rod shared with me that his parents were extremely religious and would not allow a homosexual in their house. Rod lived at home for another year and then decided to move out at age seventeen. He said that he'd rather have been on the street and true to himself than living a lie under the roof of ignorance, bigotry, and hypocrisy.

Rod told me that he believed his parents' lack of acceptance was their problem. He told me the time he spent with his parents now was very unfulfilling and distant, because they could only talk about surface things. I sensed the hurt in Rod centered around the relationship with his parents and thought back to the sudden shift in his mood when he had told me of their visit the prior week. I understood and now had compassion for this gentle and loving man.

Rod had purchased a home in Boulder six months ago and was pleased with his life for the most part. I admired this. I had heard of so many kids that had been kicked out of their homes when they told their parents that they were gay. Many of them became prostitutes, street kids, or gang members. I once read an article about a mother who had kicked her son out of the house the very day that he told her that he was gay. It was so devastating to the boy that at age sixteen, he drove his car off of a cliff. He left a note on the doorstep addressed to his mother the night of his suicide. The note was published in the local paper. It was so very sad to read. The youth's mother was now touring the country, talking to parents, and trying to educate them about loving and accepting their gay children.

I will never forget reading that article and couldn't help but think about it as I sat there with Rod. *What if this wonderful man, sitting here with me now, would have made that choice?* I would never have been blessed with meeting him.

My family wasn't great with it when I told them that I was gay, but I do remember one of my mother's first comments. "We still love you."

They never really showed it very often, but at the time, the words were enough.

We finished our lunch and made our way back to the community center and finished the envelope stuffing. Barb was so grateful for our help. I believe she thanked me personally at least four different times. I told her that I had really enjoyed my day there and offered to come back and help again. She was so pleased.

"We'd love to have you back, Drew."

Rod and I went outside. I turned to him and told him how much I enjoyed finally talking with him. I put my hand out and we shook. Rod smiled, but didn't say anything right away, and so I turned and moved towards my car.

Rod rushed over, catching me just as I was climbing into the driver's seat. "Hey, would you like to go out on a date sometime?"

"Yes," I said, without any hesitation. I was so elated that I got into my car and shut the door without discussing any further details.

Rod knocked on my car window. Now I was embarrassed. I rolled down the window, and he smiled at me. "How about Friday? Fridays are good date days!"

"Sure," I responded, barely able to hold back my excitement.

Rod told me that he would pick me up at my apartment Friday night at eight o'clock. I couldn't wait for Friday to arrive. When I think back to that day and Rod asking me out, I believe the embarrassment came from the fact that I had never had a guy ask me out on a date before. It was new for me. A part of me felt like I was still a teenager in high school.

It took me almost two hours to get ready for the date. I was so excited. I readied myself for the date and began to think about how much I had missed out on in previous years by denying this part of myself. I thought about how many times I had gone out on dates with girls just because I wanted to fit in.

I looked out my apartment window, as Rod's car pulled up to the curb. He got out of the car. He was dressed in a suit jacket. I quickly moved away from the window so that he wouldn't see me standing there. I was so nervous. The phone rang. I contemplated not answering it. I moved over to the phone and then answered it. It was Bill.

"Hey stranger."

It was so good to hear his voice. Then an almost simultaneous knock at the door. I spoke quickly into the phone. "Hey Bill, are you back? I have a date."

Bill chuckled from the other end of the phone. "He must be at the door, I'll let you go. I'm happy for you, Drew."

I hung up the phone without saying good-bye. I rushed over to the door, placed my hand on the door knob, took a quick deep breath, and opened the door.

Rod stood there. He presented me with a single red rose, which had been concealed. Never in my entire life had a guy given me a flower. I was surprised and so very touched by this gesture. I thought back to what Bill had told me about the rose and its symbolism of unconditional love. I then remembered that I had hung up on Bill. I looked at Rod and ran back to the phone and picked it up.

"Hello?"

I heard Bill's voice from the other end; he was still on the line. "Hello."

I turned away from the door, as I spoke into the phone. "You're still there?"

"I had a feeling you'd be back," Bill said.

"I'm glad you're back, and I'm sorry I hung up on you."

"I'm glad to be back. Have a great date, Drew, and I'll talk to you soon."

I said, "Good-bye," and then hung up the phone again. I looked back to the door. Rod was still standing in the doorway. I rushed over, "I'm sorry, come in."

Rod had a big grin on his face. "Drew?"

I turned, still holding the rose in my hand. "Yeah."

"It's okay."

He was able to sense how nervous I was. And yet, after he said that, it really was okay. I immediately calmed down. I moved into the kitchen and placed the rose in a vase and then placed the vase on the kitchen table. I moved back into the front room, looked at Rod. "I think I'm ready."

"You look great," he complimented.

We then went outside and Rod opened the car door for me. Another first in my experience with men. I couldn't believe it. This guy was so polite. I was no longer embarrassed or even concerned if anyone witnessed our interactions. I was enjoying this new experience. There is something about going without a thing you have longed for, for so long, that when it finally arrives, it is as if you have come home. It's as if time stops and nothing else exists. This is exactly what I was feeling at that instant. I cherished that moment in time. Rod drove us to the restaurant for dinner.

I had never eaten at The Canyon Restaurant before. It was one of the most elegant restaurants in Boulder. I was certainly glad that I had dressed appropriately. The neat thing about the restaurant was that each table was enclosed in its own private area with its own small stereo system. You could choose the type of music that you wanted to listen to, or you could bring your own. The enclosed areas were insulated, and you could rarely hear what was going on at the tables near you. This restaurant was extremely famous for their healthy vegetarian dishes as well as their seafood.

The waiter approached with what I thought was a bottle of champagne. I didn't drink because of the impact alcohol had had on my brother Frank's life and his addiction. I would have to share that with Rod. It was a nice gesture on Rod's part, but I would not be drinking any of the champagne. The waiter placed two champagne glasses on the table. I started to shake my head, "no."

"Sparkling grape juice, sir?"

"Sure," I chuckled.

Rod and I shared with each other as we sipped our sparkling grape juice. Rod didn't drink either. He never had, nor had he ever tried drugs or smoked anything. Rod had taken the sparkling grape juice to the restaurant earlier that day and had them chill it so that it would be ready for our date that evening. That impressed me. I was very much enjoying the early process of getting to know this man. Rod held his glass up to toast mine.

"Here's to a wonderful evening."

As I lowered my glass to drink, I noticed that a young teenage boy, seated at a nearby table, was craning his neck to witness the interactions between Rod and me. Rod held up his glass in the direction of the youth and winked. The boy quickly retreated back into his table. Rod seemed to be extremely comfortable with his sexuality, and he wasn't going to allow anyone to discount it. This made him even more attractive to me, not only physically, but as a strong man of character, as well.

I had broiled shrimp with organic vegetables for dinner. Rod had a wonderful display of handmade fettuccini and organic vegetables. The meal was superb. We both had a fresh fruit torte topped with homemade frozen yogurt for dessert. Almost everything in the restaurant was made from scratch. Rod told me that he had an extreme sweet tooth for desserts. I had the same weakness. We finished our dinners and made our way out of the restaurant. Rod would not allow me to pay. This was another first for me. I had always paid when out on dates. It was as if a whole new part of my life was unfolding.

After dinner, Rod drove us up Flagstaff Mountain, which flanks the west side of Boulder. There we parked and embarked on a short, mid-summer evening hike. We both agreed that the exercise would assist in the digestion of our meals.

Rod and I talked about meditation. He told me that ever since he had been kicked out of the house when he was young, he had been searching for meaning in his life. He said that his spiritual life was extremely personal but that he had connected with a greater power and this was where he obtained his inner strength and life direction. Rod said that it was important for him to make the most of his life and to be loving towards all people, which wasn't always easy. He told me that he was driven to be healthy in body, spirit, and mind and that he centered his life around living that way. He said meditation helped him to remain connected to God, an all-loving and accepting God. This was so simply put. I asked Rod about his belief in the Bible.

"I believe that there are good things in the Bible. I also believe that being gay is neither wrong nor a sin. The Bible is full of symbolism, and we can interpret in any way we choose. If we take the Bible literally, word for word, we would all be sinners. The Bible has been passed down to us as the word of God interpreted and transcribed by mankind. To me, it becomes a question of the Bible literally being 'God's word' or the 'living word' of God through mankind's eyes. What I know for sure is that my God is accepting and loving of **all** people, including people who are gay, Asian, African-American, disabled, old, young, those who have strayed from the path, everyone—every living being. I am here to live my life as best as I can. I do not force my beliefs on others and do not accept others forcing theirs on me. I only have to answer to myself and my God at the end of each day."

I enjoyed hearing what Rod shared with me. This inner strength he possessed was an extremely attractive quality.

After the hike, Rod took me back home. He walked me to the door. This was when I began to feel a bit uneasy. I wasn't sure what to do. *Do I invite him in? Do I shake his hand?* I wasn't sure.

Rod sensed my uneasiness. "Look, I think you are a sweet guy, Drew. I asked you out on a date, no strings attached. I had a great evening." He then put his hand out and smiled.

This put me at ease. I didn't know if I wanted to hug him or not. This was all so new to me. I settled for the handshake. "Thank you, Rod. I really enjoyed the evening ... as well." That was all that I said. I opened my door and went inside my apartment. Again, I felt a loving warmth inside, similar to those feelings I had after meditation or spending time with Bill. I liked Rod. That was all I knew at that point. I wrote about the evening in my notebook and then went to bed a short time later. I had an amazing dream.

Twelve

I dreamed that I was standing in the middle of a golden wheat field surrounded by large pine trees. The trees secluded this private area. The warm sun was shining above. I was lying naked in the center of the field. A beam of golden light encircled me, filling me with a feeling of total love. I felt as if I was totally protected and free in this place.

A calm and soothing voice spoke to me. "Drew you are a part of the light. You are a part of God."

I then felt my body begin to rise up and float above the field. It was as if I was wrapped in the loving light. I felt so free and protected in this place.

I remember nothing more of the dream but awoke the next morning, the sun beaming through my window, shining upon my body, casting a warm beam of light throughout my entire bedroom. I felt wonderful and refreshed.

I went for a run first thing that morning and then made my way to the bench that had become my meditation spot. I completed my premeditation ritual and then closed my eyes.

Only moments had passed when I heard a familiar voice. "Is this seat reserved?"

I opened my eyes and looked behind the bench where Bill was standing. I was so excited that I jumped up and hugged him. "I have so much to tell you."

Bill's eyes lit up as we pulled away from each other. "I bet you do."

We sat on the bench and meditated together. When the half hour ended, we both opened our eyes at precisely the same time. I felt so peaceful. Bill suggested that we take a walk.

We walked for nearly two hours. I told Bill about everything that had been happening in my life. He told me of the exciting speaking engagements he had participated in overseas. I told Bill that I had really missed him. I also told him about Rod and was excited to do so.

"Well, it's a good thing that I didn't come home sooner; you two might have never connected. Life has such a way of being spectacular!" he said.

He was right. If Bill would have come home earlier, I might never have gone to the community center and volunteered that day. I told Bill that I had been meditating regularly and that I had met my spiritual Guide but the image was a blur. Bill just smiled as if he knew something I didn't. I also told him that I had trouble remembering all that My Guide would tell me during meditations.

"Your Guide is always with you, Drew. Maybe you should use automatic writing," he suggested.

"Pardon me?" I said.

Bill continued, "Now that you have connected with your Guide, with some practice, you will be able to have conscious contact without going into full meditation. It's like having a walking meditation. Ask your Guide to be with you during the day and to present you with the correct decision in every situation."

"What is automatic writing?" I asked.

"Open up the notebook you have been writing in and ask your Guide a question. Write the question down on the paper and then ask for a written response."

"Sounds difficult," I said.

Bill replied, "It may be easier than you think. It certainly came easily for me. Maybe I was ready."

I tried to grasp what he was saying. "I just write a question and then let the pen give me the answer?"

"Exactly. It should be handwritten and you may have to close your eyes for a few moments, connecting with your Guide until you get the hang of it," Bill said.

This sounded strange to me, but I was excited to try it. Bill gave me some more information. "Your Guide has a voice of its own. You will know who is speaking on the paper. Try it tonight and start with a simple question."

"Like what?"

"I remember the first question I ever wrote to My Guide."

"What was it?" I asked.

"How do I know that there is such a thing as God?"

"What was the answer?" I asked, not being able to contain myself.

"You are a part of what you seek. The miracle of your life should only tell you so." Bill said, "I knew that wasn't me speaking, and the answer felt right even though I didn't understand the depths of it at the time."

"I don't really think that I understand."

"Practice tonight. You will receive your own answers."

We parted later that morning. I was looking forward to trying the exercise but first had to go to work. My workday seemed to progress rather slowly, because I wanted so much to get home and test the automatic writing.

One good thing about having to go to work was I told Keith that I had my first date with Rod.

"Damn, it's about time. You two would make a great couple."

"He's a great guy," I replied.

"He seems like it."

I had never had this type of conversation with anyone I worked with, and definitely not with another male. It felt good to be able to open up and discuss a delicate part of my life with someone without having to fear their judgment. I thanked Keith for being a good friend.

I went home right after work and had a small dinner, all the while staring at the notebook I had been writing in as it sat on my kitchen table. I finished my dinner and lit a small candle and placed it in the center of the table. I closed my eyes and asked My Guide to be with me. I then took a couple of deep breaths and opened my eyes. I took my notebook and opened it, and, taking pen in hand, I wrote my first question.

WHO OR WHAT IS GOD?

I waited for a moment and then placed the pen to the paper. The answer came immediately as I wrote.

A pleasure to answer this question. God is the source—all-loving, all-healing, all-present energy. It knows no judgment. God is the light and the truth. God's energy is available to all at all times. Everyone is very much a part of this powerful energy. This energy knows of no fear. All are blessed with the God energy daily. It has always been and always will be. It knows no boundaries. In short, God is love. I was pleased with the answer, although I didn't totally understand the lawyerly response, but I continued on and wrote another question.

IS THERE MORE THAN ONE GOD?

God, at its source, is love. It is all-encompassing and therefore there is only one God and that God is defined as love. It is an energy and is ever present. It is much like your earthly experience of gravity. It is everywhere but you are unable to see it; yet, know it is there. You only understand it when you allow yourself to be aware of its existence. Many want to think that there is more than one God. Who and what they pray to are but symbols, and for them, they are correct in doing so.

The answers were flowing as easily as Bill had suggested. Maybe I was ready too. I continued my questioning.

BUT I WAS TAUGHT TO BELIEVE IN A GOD UP THERE. WAS THIS WRONG?

This was not wrong, for God knows no judgment. This was a basis for your own spiritual journey. You are now further ahead on your journey. As one grows spiritually, so do one's beliefs. Beliefs then, may begin to change, sometimes daily.

DOES GOD HATE GAY PEOPLE?

The God energy, as you have been told, is love. There is no judgment. Love is all-encompassing and knows nothing else. The energy of God is ***only*** *love and knows nothing of what is called hate.*

WHAT ABOUT CRIME?

You are a spiritual being in human form. You are now experiencing a physical existence. One of the gifts bestowed upon you in the physical world is the gift of "free will." What this means is that you are very much in control of your own life on Earth as are all others. Some choose a life of crime.

WHAT IS IT THAT WE HAVE FREE WILL OVER?

Your entire life. You may not think so at times. You have free will to choose how you are to act, react, and think, in every life situation. This includes your emotional responses, as well.

I HAVE CONTROL OVER MY EMOTIONS?

Yes. For example, if someone has made an appointment with you and they do not show up, you have the choice to be accepting of the circumstances from a place of nonjudgment or you may choose to judge it and feel anger. You may also choose to be hurt. In every moment, and in every situation, how you respond is your choice. These are three possible emotional responses to only one situation. Many do not believe that there is a choice, but you are reminded that free will always exists.

All on the Earth plane have placed themselves right where they find themselves in any given moment. When situations such as the one we have just mentioned arise, often blame is put on another individual. Many times, we may not know where the other person is on their spiritual journey.

BUT DON'T SOME PEOPLE TRY TO HURT OTHERS INTENTIONALLY?

Remember free will and choice. Some may choose to try and hurt others.

WHY DO THEY DO THIS?

It is generally that they are operating out of a place of fear. This we can equate to operating out of a place of darkness or partial light. Fear can be abundant in locations around the Earth plane. Many of those operating out of a place of fear have forgotten who they are. The fear or darkness can be replaced.

REPLACED WITH WHAT?

The first choice would be that of love or light. Where this can exist and be all-encompassing, there can be no opposite. Our natural state is to operate from love or light. Many have chosen a different route out of fear. This is usually from holding on to past situations they have experienced on the Earth plane.

I DO NOT UNDERSTAND.
WHAT DO YOU MEAN BY THIS?

We all have situations in our lives where we have chosen to be hurt. Until we have truly forgiven ourselves and others, we may remain stuck there. We need to move on from the situation, and until we do, we may carry the emotions of hurt or anger with us into our next earthly encounter. It will usually surface in a similar situation. When this happens, we are then living in the past and have forgotten to live in the present moment.

I THINK I UNDERSTAND, BUT PLEASE EXPLAIN.

The best example is in the area of human relationships. If you have been intimately involved with another in the past and this person left you or ended the relationship without explanation or reason, you may have chosen to be angry or hurt. We need to remind ourselves that we do not always know where the other individual is on their spiritual journey. Unless we choose to handle the situation from a place of love and acceptance and know that the Universe is always in divine order, we will react.

We need to remember that what we have created in our lives is moving us forward on our journey. If we do not accept this, we may then carry a past experience forward. The next time that we are involved intimately in a relationship, we may choose to be on guard or fearful that the individual we are currently with is going to leave us, as well. This prevents us from experiencing the moment and will affect our current situation. A past situation may keep us from getting involved again, unless we let go.

Remember, we are all works in progress.

HOW DO WE KEEP FROM CHOOSING TO BE HURT?

It is not always easy. There may be a lesson for us to learn. The key is to feel what we choose to feel, bless the situation, and move on, without judgment. Do not ignore your feelings. Feelings are your "emotional guidance system." There are certainly times when anger and sadness are the most appropriate of choices concerning the emotional world. We are here for the human experience, but at our core, we are spiritual beings of love and light.

I was beginning to feel slightly overwhelmed and so I placed my pen down and closed my notebook. There was so much information coming forth so quickly. It was amazing. I thought about the word choice. *Did I truly choose how I would react in every situation in my life? And if I did make these choices, were there any choices that I had made in the past that were keeping me from truly living in the present? Was I holding on to things in the past?* I knew the answer was probably "yes." I just didn't know if I wanted to go back and look. I thought about this briefly. I knew that in this moment I had the choice to either go back into past memories or not. It was as if in this very moment a lesson was presenting itself to me. *Maybe it was one that would make my life better?* Another thought occurred. *Maybe we have the choice as to whether or not we are to grow in spirit and healing in any given moment?* I knew the answer was "yes." I immediately thought about a past intimate relationship. Maybe there was something in that relationship that I was still holding on to that was holding me back from having the next relationship. I decided to go for a hike and ask My Guide for some assistance in seeing what this could be.

Thirteen

I drove to Chautauqua—a beautiful park that lies near the foot of the Flatiron Mountains in Boulder—and started hiking. The air was crisp. Being in this beautiful place, I felt my connection with the grandness and beauty of the Universe. I looked to the mountains in their beautiful glory and thought, *How could there not be a God?* I continued to hike and reminisced about a past relationship I had had with a girl named Shelly.

I had met Shelly in college. She was Ryan's sister. He was one of my best friends. Shelly was still in high school when we met. Ryan introduced us, and we hit it off immediately. We dated for almost two years and had a great relationship. This was the last woman that I had seriously dated before realizing that I was gay. The end of our relationship was extremely painful. I had struggled with accepting my sexual orientation for some time. The guy that I caught staring at me in college at the library was really attractive. I couldn't help but stare back that day. I was planning to be with Shelly the same night sexually, but all I could think about was the guy from the library. It was soon after that I began to withdraw from her. She would ask me what was bothering me, and I wouldn't even respond. Shelly became extremely frustrated with me, because I was avoiding her. I eventually told her that the relationship wasn't working and gave her no further explanation. I ended our relationship and disappeared from her life.

At the time, I lived in an apartment with two other guys. Shelly would call, and I would hang up on her. I told my roommates not to give Shelly any information about me. I even began to retreat from them. One day Shelly called, and I answered the phone. She was crying and asked me what it was that she had done. I said nothing and hung up the phone. I moved out of the apartment soon after that and didn't even tell my roommates where I was moving.

I dated very few women after that. I would go out with a woman once or twice, but that would be it.

I shut myself off from the idea of dating guys. I was too fearful. I knew how badly I had hurt Shelly. I felt so much turmoil around my sexuality that I could not begin to discuss it with anyone, much less her.

Thinking about how I'd handled the situation with Shelly brought up feelings of sadness and anger. I was angry at myself for not being man enough to tell her the truth, and I was sad that I had hurt her.

I began to think about the information that I had been given through the automatic writing, about how we have the power to choose our emotional responses. I was choosing these feelings now in this moment, and I needed to let them go. Maybe I had been choosing to carry these feelings with me as a sort of punishment ever since my relationship with Shelly ended. I sat down on a secluded rock, took out my notebook, and wrote a question to My Guide.

WHAT DO I NEED TO DO TO COMPLETE MY RELATIONSHIP WITH SHELLY IN ORDER TO MOVE ON?

The answer came immediately.

Drew, contacting Shelly may be the answer. Communication is the key. You may choose to tell her the truth. This will allow you to bless the past situation and move on.

Could it be that simple? I got up and made my way down the trail. I rushed home and searched for Shelly's phone number. It had been two years since I had disappeared from her life. I found her number, picked up the phone, and dialed. As amazing as it sounds, she answered the phone. The minute that I said it was Drew, she hung up. I immediately called back, and she picked up the phone again. "Drew, don't call. I don't want to talk to you, ever again," she said, hanging up once again.

I was shocked. *What was I to do now?* I needed more information. I took out my notebook and transcribed another question for My Guide.

HOW DO I COMPLETE SOMETHING ALONE?

You can write a letter to the individual if they were not receptive to a face-to-face completion. You do not need to mail the letter. You are writing it for you. It is a way to write out the feelings you have about a past situation, to apologize. It can be extremely freeing.

Another technique is to go into meditation with your Guide and ask the other individual or individuals to join you there. It is important to go to a safe place. You will have the protection of your Guide. You then may share with the individual what it is that you wanted to share in person. With the support of your Guide, ask the individual for feedback. Listen to what it is that they have to say. Thank them and then bless them. Bless yourself as well. Thank yourself for sharing the truth. Wish the other party well on their journey. Offer them and yourself love and thank yourself once again for the work that you have done. Emerge from the meditation. It is that simple.

It did seem simple but not easy. I took a few deep breaths, closed my eyes and then asked My Guide to join me.

A warm, translucent presence appeared, comforting but still unrecognizable. I was in a safe place, the golden field of wheat, surrounded by pine trees. I asked the Universe to invite Shelly to join us. From the pine trees that surrounded the field, she appeared. She looked as beautiful as I remembered her, brunette hair, athletic. She walked over and stood in front of me.

I began to speak to Shelly. I told her about how sorry I was for walking out on her and told her that it wasn't anything she had done. I told her I had been afraid for a long time. I told her that I was gay and had been struggling with it. I then invited her to share. She told me that I had hurt her deeply. A tear fell from her eye. She just stood there as did I. I moved towards her and embraced her. I thanked her for sharing with me. I felt My Guide's presence behind me. I moved back and wished her only love and blessed her on her life's journey. Shelly turned and walked out of the field and then disappeared into the pine trees.

I opened my eyes. I had been crying. I wiped the tears from my eyes and then took a few deep breaths. I felt complete and at peace with Shelly. I thanked My Guide and then blessed and thanked myself for doing this work. I then drove back to my apartment.

A friend who had visited Taos, New Mexico, had given me a smudge stick made of sage. I went to my bedroom where I had kept the sage in a drawer. I had never used it but had been told that sage was very cleansing. I lit the smudge stick and encircled my body with the smoking herb. I then extinguished the sage and made my way outside to sit on my balcony. I sat there, looking to the boldness of the Flatirons in the distance, reflecting on the exercise that I had just completed. I knew that I had just been given an invaluable tool to use in healing any and all of the past relationships in my life that still seemed to be unresolved. What a gift. I felt as if my life was becoming more and more complete. I felt such a sense of freedom in that moment. I felt so alive in spirit. It was as if I was shedding an old skin and being guided to live my life in true harmony, fully appreciating the present moment.

When I went back into my apartment, I noticed the answering machine blinking. I retrieved the message. It was from Bill. "Drew, this is Bill, you must be hiking. I would love to get together with you for lunch tomorrow. Hey, if you have no plans tonight, I have a suggestion. I have a great friend, a doctor, Dr. Luke, at Children's Hospital in Denver. He's a special guy. Why don't you go spend the evening with him. He is expecting you. Please call and let me know if you are available for lunch tomorrow. I would like to connect with you before I leave town again."

Bill had called while I was hiking. *How did he know I was hiking?* It's as if he was in tune with my entire life. *How does he have the energy to travel as much as he does?* I really wanted to see Bill before he left town again. I wasn't sure about visiting Children's Hospital that night. *Why did he want me to visit a doctor?*

Fourteen

Somewhat reluctantly, I made my way from Boulder to Denver. I arrived at Children's Hospital, completing the drive in forty-five minutes. I walked into the hospital and approached a woman at the main reception/check-in desk on the first floor.

"I would like to see Dr. Luke, please."

The woman looked at me strangely. She then glanced over at her coworker, who was standing by her side.

"He's here to see Dr. Luke!" They both started laughing, turned away from me and ducked behind the desk for a brief instant.

I didn't understand what was going on.

The women then popped up, simultaneously,

facing me now and both wearing black plastic glasses adorned with fake noses and mustaches. One had a rubber cigar in her hand. She proceeded to speak to me in a Groucho Marx voice. "He's upstairs, sweetheart, fourth floor."

"Thanks," I replied, I'm sure with a very puzzled look on my face. I moved away, and both women continued to play and laugh hysterically.

I rode the elevator up to the fourth floor, wondering as I ascended, *Am I on my way to the Psychiatric Unit?*

The door opened on the fourth floor. It was as if a curtain had just risen on a circus scene. The entire floor was painted in very bright and playful colors. There were balloons everywhere. The doctors and nurses had on colorful and fun scrubs. If not for their identification badges, it would have been hard to recognize them as professionals.

I moved towards the fourth floor reception desk. The nurse on duty had her back to me.

"Hello. My name is Drew Wilson, and I am here to see Dr. Luke."

The nurse immediately turned around. She had a clown nose on, bright red. I laughed.

"Just what are you laughing at?" she asked.

I stopped laughing. "I'm sorry."

"Sorry? Why?" She then squeezed a rubber horn that hung from around her waist. It honked as she stood up to face me. "Laughing is the law of the fourth floor!" She smiled at me. "And, Dr. Luke swears by it." She then pointed down the hallway. "Room #412, Drew Wilson."

"Thank you." I turned and made my way down the hallway.

"Hey," the nurse yelled. "You'll need this."

I stopped and turned around. Just as I did, she threw something red at me, which bounced off of my chest and landed in my hands. It was a red clown nose. I wrinkled my forehead, looked back at the nurse, who was now pointing to hers.

"Put it on."

I chuckled again, and put the clown nose on. I made my way to room #412. It was about halfway down the hall on the left side. I approached the door and knocked softly. I heard a television set playing on the other side of the door. It sounded like a cartoon.

"Come in," spoke a child's voice.

I slowly opened the door to witness a room filled with balloons, stuffed animals, flowers, and a small boy about twelve years old lying in bed. He had no hair and looked pale and sickly, which made him seem older than he was. A doctor was in the room seated on the bed next to the frail boy.

The young boy was intently watching the cartoon on the screen opposite his bed. Just as I entered the room, he burst into laughter. I briefly looked at the television. A *Roadrunner* cartoon was playing. The coyote had just gone over the cliff and landed, a puff of smoke rising after his hard fall. I looked to the doctor.

"Dr. Luke?" The doctor stood up.

"No."

"I'm sorry, I must have the wrong room." I turned to leave.

"Hey," the little boy spoke. I turned around to see the young boy standing on his bed now, bouncing up and down. "I'm Dr. Luke!"

I shook my head in disbelief.

"And I'm a clown," I said.

The young boy started laughing hysterically. "I know."

"Okay, Dr. Luke, time to lie down," said the physician. The young boy sat back down in his bed as the physician approached me. He pulled a clown nose out of his pocket and put it on.

"Can I speak to you privately, one clown to another?"

We both started laughing. We moved outside of the room, and Dr. Luke continued to laugh as he watched the *Bugs Bunny and Roadrunner Show* on the television. The physician took me to a nearby waiting area, and we sat down on two bean bag chairs. *I hadn't sat in a bean bag chair in years,* I chuckled to myself.

"I was told ... "

"I know," the physician spoke. "Bill told me you would be coming by to visit. Bill spends quite a bit of time with the children here. He loves being around kids. Dr. Luke is his favorite."

The physician, who told me to call him Dr. John, then explained to me that Luke, a.k.a., Dr. Luke, had been at the hospital off and on over the past few years. The young boy had leukemia, and his name really was Luke. His father was a wealthy entrepreneur and also a physician who believed in the power of humor and lectured around the country to other physicians on the healing power of humor and laughter. When his son was diagnosed with leukemia, he donated a huge sum of money to the hospital with the stipulation that it be used for what he called "humor therapy."

"We've had a number of spontaneous remissions here since then."

"What does that mean?" I asked.

"It's the medical profession's way of saying, 'We don't know how the hell to explain it, but kids are getting better.'"

"That's great," I smiled at Dr. John.

"We think so." Dr. John attempted to stand up, having some difficulty getting out of his bean bag chair. "Let's go join the kids for ice cream."

"Cool."

I, too, had some difficulty getting out of my bean bag chair. My clown nose fell off, and Dr. John retrieved it, tossing it back to me.

"Don't forget your visitor pass."

I put the nose back on and laughed as we moved down the hallway towards another room. Everyone we passed—staff, visitors, patients, you name it—had clown noses on. Each one was smiling and laughing. I had ice cream with the kids and Dr. John and then spent some time with "Dr. Luke."

Dr. Luke and I watched cartoons. The *Bugs Bunny and Roadrunner Show* was his favorite. Dr. Luke had an infectious laugh, which, in turn, caused me to laugh.

I thought it interesting and strange that every time the coyote would go over the cliff and fall, ending with a puff of smoke, Dr. Luke would laugh. I didn't laugh.

"We never die," Dr. Luke said one time after this happened. "Just like the coyote never dies."

"What?" I responded.

"I love cartoons; they're funny," Luke said next. "Don't you like to laugh, Drew?"

I did, and for the next thirty minutes, Dr. Luke challenged me to a laughing contest. He ended up winning but invited me to come back anytime for a rematch. I didn't think I had ever laughed so much in my entire life.

A nurse came into Luke's room at 9:00 p.m. She was large. Her clown nose looked so small on her robust and chubby face. "Bedtime in five minutes, Dr. Luke."

"Okay," Luke responded and then accidently passed some gas. It wasn't quiet. Dr. Luke looked at me and started laughing. I then started to laugh. The nurse tried to fight back her laughter but couldn't, and she started laughing too.

"Five minutes," the nurse waved, trying to clear the smell from the air in an animated gesture, and then left Dr. Luke's room.

"I'm gonna be a doctor when I grow up."

"Cool," I said.

"What are you gonna be?"

I hesitated, and Dr. Luke spoke again.

"Or, maybe I'll be a fireman. It doesn't matter, I guess, as long as you can laugh and be happy and really enjoy what you are doing."

This young boy deeply touched my soul that night. I really enjoyed the evening and was so happy that I had made the decision to visit Dr. Luke. Bill must have known what an impression this amazing boy would have on me.

After arriving home, I called Bill. The phone rang a few times, and then, Nancy answered. She had been sleeping. I apologized for waking her, but explained how I just had to speak with Bill to thank him. She woke Bill, and gave him the phone. Bill delivered a groggy, "Hello?" I apologized to him, as well, but said that I just had to thank him for setting up the appointment with Dr. Luke.

"I thought you would enjoy yourself. Are we on for lunch tomorrow?"

"You bet."

I once again apologized for waking him and Nancy. Bill chuckled and told me that he had expected a late night call from me and even told Nancy so before they went to sleep.

"I'll pick you up tomorrow at noon."

Bill just always seemed to know exactly what I needed in order to take the next step on my journey. What an awesome being Bill was.

Fifteen

I hardly slept that night, so grateful for the time with Dr. Luke. Having a sense of humor and not taking life so seriously all of the time was the gift he had given to me. I arose early and went for my run and then proceeded to meditate. My Guide shared some information with me, although I did not know at the time exactly what the information meant.

"Your life is becoming everything that you truly wish it to be."

I came out of the meditation and remembered exactly what the message was. I had a feeling that I was in for some more changes. I began to think about my job and wondered again where it was that I saw myself in five years. And, at this point, I wasn't sure if I saw myself at my current job. This was frightening to me. I had spent four years in college preparing myself to do what I was now doing for work. I had really thought that I wanted to be involved in the fitness industry for my life's work, but now, slight doubts were surfacing.

I got ready for work and arrived at the club to be greeted at the front door by Janet's smiling face.

"Drew, could I speak with you as soon as you get settled in?"

"Sure." I had a feeling from this unique greeting by the owner that something was up. It didn't take long for me to get settled in at work.

Janet walked into her office, and in a few minutes, I followed. Janet stood as I entered the office and asked if I would like something to drink. I declined the offer, and then she asked me to close the door, which I did. I sat down across from her, not feeling the least bit nervous or threatened. I thought of past interactions such as this, realizing they usually made me extremely nervous. Maybe my utter calm was a result of the meditation that I had been practicing.

Janet began to speak. "Drew, I just wanted to thank you for all your help and hard work during your short course of employment here at the club. I have come to honor you as one of our most valued employees. I don't believe that there is a member or an employee in this club that doesn't just adore you." Janet paused for a moment and placed a green folder in front of me, "I'd like to offer you an assistant manager position."

I was extremely surprised and had no clue as to what to say. If this had been a short time ago, I would have said "yes" without even thinking. I knew that there was no assistant manager at the club currently and that meant that they were creating a new position for me. I also had those immediate thoughts of "where I saw myself in five years," and I still didn't know. I opened my mouth and was surprised what came out. "Can I think about it?"

Janet was taken aback slightly. "Sure," she said. "How much time do you need?"

I wasn't really sure, but I thought that the one person I wanted to consult with about this was Bill, and I knew that we were to have lunch that very day. "How about a week?"

Janet honored my request. She then reached over and opened up the green folder that rested on the desk in front of me. "You would be the youngest person in management at the club. We have created this new position to spread the workload out and have also included within your new position, if you choose to take it, a quarterly review of the facility and its operations. A suggestion prompted by your research. The pay is $42,000 per year with full benefits, medical and dental, one month of vacation and profit sharing."

I was amazed by the generosity of the offer. *How could I wait?* But, I needed to. Janet was to take a one-week vacation to attend a seminar in Florida beginning the next day. We agreed to meet when she returned.

About an hour before Bill and I had planned to meet for lunch, Rod walked into the club. I had not seen him or heard from him since our date. It was pleasing to see him once again. He walked up to the front counter and smiled at me. I smiled back. There was a new girl, Meagan, working at the front desk, and she was studying the interactions between us. I'm sure that Rod picked up on this, because he only handed me his membership card and then moved quickly past. I turned to Meagan.

"Is he gay or something?" She asked, casting a disgusted look in his direction.

I was amused by her ignorance. "Why don't you go ask him?"

Her next response only added to my perception

of her as ignorant. "It's too bad if he is. He is so good looking."

I said nothing. Meagan was only nineteen and was at the club for a summer internship, which was soon to end. I realized that I was judging her reaction to the situation and that whenever I was confronted with a judgment about sexuality, I tended to judge back. I didn't treat her any differently for her beliefs, nor did I try to change them, and saying nothing seemed the best way to go about doing that.

Bill came into the club a short time later. I was extremely excited to go to lunch with him. Meagan watched as Bill approached the front desk. "Are you going to lunch with your grandfather?"

I looked at her and chuckled. "No, he's a friend."

"He is awfully old to be a friend," she whispered.

I stepped out to greet Bill, amused by Meagan's previous comments. I was extremely honored to call Bill my friend.

We made our way to the health food store and deli. This was Bill's favorite place and was quickly becoming one of mine. I had also spoken highly of it to many club employees and members. I could tell that Bill sensed that something was up with me, so I didn't waste any time. "They just offered me a new position at the club," I said, as we sat down at a table outside.

"That's wonderful, Drew." He was so genuine and sincere.

"I told Janet that I would like to think about it. It's like the entire life I have dreamed about is now happening. I have always participated in sports and enjoyed fitness. I eventually want to own my own club. But now, with this opportunity to move another step closer to that goal, I'm unsure for some reason.

"This guy, Rod, is really great. I don't know him that well, but I really like him. He came into the club today just before you did. Meagan, our new intern, asked me if Rod was gay. It's like a part of me wanted to tell her yes, and another part wanted to tell her that it wasn't any of her business. I thought about telling her that I was gay, and then I thought that it didn't matter. I'm really confused."

Bill turned around for a moment, his face out of sight. I wondered what he was doing.

"Bill?" I said.

A few seconds passed, and then he turned back around, his nose adorned with a dented, old, red, clown nose. I immediately began to laugh, then retrieved mine from my jacket pocket and put it on. We both laughed.

"Drew, sometimes when life gets to be too much, you just have to laugh and not take things so seriously."

I nodded in total agreement. After a few more moments of laughter, the conversation shifted.

"Are you able to take a week away from your job?" Bill finished the last bite of his sandwich.

"For what?"

"I have a small cabin near Rocky Mountain National Park just outside of Estes Park. If you are willing, I think you should try something."

I didn't know where Bill was coming from. At this point, the last thing I wanted was another assignment, and with his clown nose still on, it was hard to take him seriously. "Are you serious? I don't understand."

Bill leaned in and took off his clown nose, and I followed suit. "Yes. We are all presented with many challenging decisions at certain times in our lives. It is like you have arrived at a crossroads in your life. It happens to us all on many different levels. You are on two journeys here—a physical one and a spiritual one. At times, the two come into conflict with one another, and it is at those times that we most need to go inside and ask what direction is best for us to move in."

"I feel like I am going crazy," I said.

"That's good," Bill chuckled.

"Good? How can it be good?"

"Good, because it shows that you are present with your life. Many people in this situation would just continue to move forward, so quickly that they would never take the time to stop and contemplate what direction they truly wanted to move in. Oftentimes, when we slow down and take the time to find out what direction we really want to go, we find out that it is actually 180 degrees from where we were headed. That's when we need to listen to our heart, our spirit."

"But how do you make the right decision?" I asked.

Bill sat straight up and looked me directly in the eyes. "Drew, you will know."

I took a moment and went inside to use the health food store's rest room. Back outside, and feeling a bit more at ease, I sat down again with Bill. "Okay, I feel better," I said, smiling at Bill.

Bill smiled back and offered some encouraging words. "I suggest that you go back to work and ask your boss if you could take a week away from the club to think about the job offer. Go to the grocery store and buy a week's worth of food. Gather your pen and notebook and go up to my cabin, alone. You'll have a little end-of-the-summer vacation and be able to spend the week with nature, not talking to anyone while you are there."

"Why?"

Bill continued, "So that you can listen to your true inner voice, your highest spirit, away from all distractions."

The thought of complete seclusion made me feel uncomfortable. "I don't know if I can do that. I don't know if she will give me the time off."

Bill sensed my fear and he responded with love. "Drew, there is nothing to be afraid of. You have been preparing for this. If your boss truly wants you for this position and if you are to truly have it, nothing will stand in the way of your receiving it. But, you need to love yourself enough to make the correct decision." Bill placed his hand gently upon my shoulder, and I felt instantly grounded and relaxed.

I thought for a few moments about this next challenge. Spending an entire week alone, not speaking to anyone. I enjoyed the mountains, but the thought of going crazy out in the middle of a forest didn't seem attractive to me. Soon after I had this thought, a sense of calm passed through my entire body. I felt the presence of My Guide.

Bill spoke as if on Universal cue. "You should use the time you are there to ask your Guide anything and everything that you have wondered about your life and your true place in the Universe. The insight you gain will serve as a foundation for the rest of your life."

"I should do it." I knew at that moment that I needed to go.

"I'm leaving town again as well," Bill said.

"Where are you going now?"

"Quebec, Canada."

"Don't you ever get tired of traveling?" I asked.

"I miss Nancy when I am gone, but I really enjoy the work that I do. Drew, there was a time years ago when I thought that I should retire. I was very seriously contemplating canceling a speaking engagement in Utah. I was to speak at a small camp for troubled young adults. Something inside told me that I needed to go and speak, and that if afterwards, I still wanted to retire and quit traveling, it would be fine. But for some unknown reason, I just had to speak to that very group of kids."

"You went then?"

"Yes, and I was there for three days. I spent a fair amount of time with those kids. There was one boy there, Marcus; he was eighteen years old and extremely quiet. He would sit way in the back during all of my talks and presentations. I never spoke with him one-on-one but smiled at him when he gave me the slightest bit of his attention. The other kids left him alone. The night before I was to leave, I gave a talk about dreams. I told the kids about my life as a salesman and how much I enjoyed helping others to fulfill their dreams of buying a new car. I also told the kids a story that I do not often share. It was about my younger sister, Jessica."

I had never known that Bill had a sister.

"Jessica was the most beautiful girl, and I was very blessed to have had her as a sister. Jessica was walking home alone after school one day. I was supposed to be with her, but had decided to disobey my parents. I went and played with some of my friends that day instead." Bill stopped and then swallowed, "She was hit by an automobile and killed while crossing the street near our house. The man driving the car had had a heart attack while driving. She was killed instantly. This was extremely hard on my family, especially my mother. I was eighteen at the time, just about the age of Marcus, the quiet boy at the camp. I wondered how God could have allowed my sister to be killed and was angry at God and myself for a very long time. Through it all, my parents never blamed me once for what happened. But I blamed myself. I was going to take my life because I just couldn't make sense of the tragedy.

"I decided that I would hang myself from the ceiling rafter in my room one day while my parents were away from home. I made a noose the best that I knew how and slung the rope over a strong beam in my bedroom. I stood on a chair, secured the rope on the beam, and then placed the noose around my neck. Then something amazing happened, I kicked the chair out from underneath my feet and immediately the rope broke, sending me crashing to the floor. I twisted my ankle.

"I sat on the floor for a few minutes and began to think about my sister. I don't know if it was an angel or my sister, but there she was, standing right above me as I sat on the floor, grasping my right ankle. She was wearing one of her favorite dresses, and she was laughing at me. My deceased sister was laughing at me!

"I was so confused, then she spoke, 'Billy, why are you trying to do all of the world's work? It isn't your time yet. You have so many great things to do. That rope was as destined to break as I was to go.' We cannot interfere with the Universal divine plan. I was eighteen years old, and to this day, I still remember what she said. I never told my parents about that sacred moment. I examined the rope afterwards and it looked as if it had been cut straight through.

"Things turned around for me after that day. I started to think about everything differently. I decided I should accept things as they are if I cannot change them and that sometimes things happen in our earthly existence and we may never know why. I began to feel valuable as a human being, that I was here to do something important. I didn't know what at that time, but I just held on to the belief.

"I shared with the kids that we are all here to do valuable things and that God is watching out for us, even when we may not think so.

"Well, as I was leaving the camp, Marcus followed me out to my rental car. He stopped me, 'Mr. Gustafson, Sir?' I turned around. Marcus continued, 'I would like to thank you for being here this weekend. You see, my little brother, Jamie, died about a year ago. I had always thought that it was my fault. We were both riding our bikes one day, and Jamie got his shoelace stuck in his bike chain. He looked down to pull it out and swerved into traffic and was hit by an oncoming car. I yelled, but not in time. I thought that it was my fault, that I should have died. I tried to cut up my wrists, and my parents sent me up here. Last night, I was thinking about Jamie and how much I missed him. I was going to kill myself with a knife from the kitchen. For some reason, I decided to hear you speak, and now I don't want to. I want to live.' The boy then started to cry. I held him and told him it was okay.

"I left the camp that day and now make it back there every single year, and have for about twenty years. There is a teacher there, a Mr. Steiner. He is one of my favorites. He is also very much one of the camps favorites as well. He receives awards and praise from the school, the county, and he even received an accommodation from the president of the United States. You see, Mr. Steiner was that little boy. Marcus, Marcus Steiner."

I was touched deeply by the story that Bill had just shared with me. We finished our lunch and then made our way back to the club. Bill handed me the directions and a key to his small cabin and wished me good luck with my decision. I wished him well on his excursion to Quebec and watched from the entrance to the club as Bill drove away.

I went inside and walked directly towards Janet's office. I was slightly nervous about requesting the week off, knowing that she was leaving town as well, but I shouldn't have been. I asked her if I could take the next week off so that I could truly decide what I wanted to do—not only with her job offer, but also with my life. I told her that I needed the time to determine the direction that I wanted my life to take both professionally and personally.

The response she gave was only one word. "Certainly."

After work, I packed and readied myself to leave for the cabin. I would be leaving that same evening. As I was packing, there was a knock at my door. I opened it and saw Rod standing there. I was pleased to see him, and he looked surprised to see me with my backpack in hand.

"Are you moving?"

I chuckled at the frightened look on his face. "No," I said.

"Good," he responded, the look on his face giving way to relief.

I told Rod that I was going to take a week away by myself at Bill's cabin outside of Estes Park by myself, but I didn't share my fears with him. He asked if I wanted to have dinner with him that evening, and I agreed.

We drove separately to a Chinese restaurant, because I was going to drive up to the cabin after dinner. My backpack was in the back of the car, stuffed with food, clothing, and my notebook.

Rod was quiet at dinner. I was not very talkative myself. We both ordered—a chicken dish and a vegetable dish. I was quiet because I was really afraid of spending an entire week alone with myself and my thoughts. I was sure that it would be a transforming experience, but I still had the fear. My silence was in preparation for the time I would be spending alone. I'm sure I seemed shut down from Rod's perspective. I sat there eating and thinking quite a bit. I thought about Rod and looked at him and smiled, as I thought about our previous date. I knew that I did not want to advance in our relationship until I returned from my trip but did not verbalize this to Rod. Rod broke the ice about halfway through the dinner. "Hey, are you attracted to me?"

"Yes, I am," was my immediate response.

Rod returned a smile. I didn't know what to say next. Rod did. "Good. Because I really like you. I'm glad that you started talking to me at the gym. I had been checking you out for quite a while there."

"Really?"

"Yes," Rod nodded his head.

"I was doing the same thing."

Rod smiled again.

I wanted to keep the conversation light and was also anxious to get up to the cabin before dark, so I finished my meal quickly and then looked at my watch. "I want to get up there before it gets dark," I said.

Rod nodded in support of my plans. We both finished and arose from the table.

Outside, I moved towards my car and Rod followed. I sensed that there was something that he still wanted to say to me. I was right. I opened my car door and then Rod moved closer. "How about a hug?"

I turned back and smiled. I had never had anyone ask me for a hug before. These were the types of things that I liked about Rod. He seemed to be very considerate about not pushing me for anything. We hugged. It felt nice to experience the warmth and touch of another individual, especially one that I was attracted to. We pulled back from each other.

"I would really like to go out with you again when I get back," I said.

"I would too," Rod said.

He held the door for me as I got into my car. Rod closed the car door and stepped back. He watched as I pulled out of the parking space and waved to me as I drove off.

Sixteen

I drove from Boulder for about an hour and a half, and I was there. With Bill's directions, I had no trouble finding the secluded cabin. I unlocked the door and went inside. It was extremely small, one room basically. There was no electricity. An old woodstove sat on the east side, with plenty of wood stacked up next to it. There was a large cooler on the floor on the north side of the cabin. A spacious bed adorned the west wall, overflowing with blankets and pillows. A small, two-person table sat in the middle of the room. There were two chairs, one on either side. Candles had been placed everywhere there was a flat surface.

It seemed like a nice place to get away from city life, but it wasn't a place I'd want to be during the cold winter months. It felt great to escape the extreme heat of August in Boulder.

Bill had told me that there were a couple of hiking trails within a few hundred yards of the cabin. One went directly to Donner Lake, and the other headed towards an open field. I definitely wanted to visit both places while I was there. I had checked out the local weather reports before I left Boulder, and it was forecast to be nice the entire time I was to be at the cabin.

I had decided to stay up for awhile and write to My Guide. I had a number of questions to ask. I lit a candle and placed it on a small end table next to the bed. I climbed up on the huge bed with my pen and notebook. I put pen to paper and began to write.

WILL I BE ABLE TO MAKE IT THROUGH A WEEK WITHOUT HUMAN CONTACT?

Drew, you will. It will not always be easy, but you come from discipline. The benefits of your time here will last a lifetime. The time you are to spend here will also be time that will assist you in the reshaping of your life. You will discover your true inner beliefs. You will learn on a very deep level much of who you truly are. You will also discover beliefs that you may now not be aware of. Honor yourself for having the courage and strength to undertake this journey.

I AM FRIGHTENED. WHY?

The fear stems from the unknown. This time here is a new practice for you, and fear would be normal for many of us in a similar situation. Honor yourself for allowing the fear to surface and to continue your journey in spite of the fear. Be assured of the great benefits that you will derive from this time. Know on the highest of levels that you are not at all alone in this place. You are with your true Guide.

WHAT AM I TO LEARN IN THIS PLACE?

On the highest of levels, you are here to learn about a part of you that has been neglected, your inner Guide—the part of you that is the light which has been spoken of—the love that is at the core of your being. It is your God energy and it is your true strength. It is that energy in you that is all-knowing and all-loving. You will go as deep to your core of love as you are willing to discover. It is your inner Guide that has led you this far, and it longs to lead you to your core.

I then asked what turned out to be a premature question.

DO I TAKE THE JOB PROMOTION AT THE HEALTH CLUB?

You will have the answer to that question as time progresses. Telling you the answer at this point would call for a reaction on your part. Rest assured, the answer to this question will come later.

I knew that I had asked the question prematurely, as did My Guide. I didn't understand what My Guide had meant about having a "reaction" to the answer but I let it go. I was very much on the fence about what to do regarding the offer. I didn't truly know what I wanted for myself for my future at this point. I was also tired, and so I asked one final question.

WHY WAS I BORN GAY?

Drew, this was a soul choice before you arrived on the Earth plane. Do not confuse this with the choices that you make once you are delivered into this world in human form. You incarnated in this life as a gay man. If people only knew how many times we have all been here—it would humor them to know that we have all been male, female, gay, and nongay, many times over. It is interesting how much of an issue is made over sexuality and skin color on the Earth plane.

Your deepest purpose here is to love your fellow humans, be they gay or nongay or of any color, race, creed, religion, and so on. Love is love.

You have had a struggle for so long with the issue of being gay. Your lesson is to accept who you are completely and let it be. Remember the speech your friend Bill gave to you months ago in that college class about what it is that we are all here to do. We are here "to be ourselves and to share that with others." Your being gay is a part of who you are. So many gay individuals let the fear of letting that fact out interfere with allowing others to know anything about them. This is in itself a lesson. There are those in our lives who love us unconditionally and accept us for who we are. They accept everything about us. This is the true message of love.

Unconditional love is something that we must first have for ourselves, and then and only then, can we have it for another. This is something to look for when connecting with another. Many individuals who are homosexual have difficulty loving themselves. This is another lesson to be learned. Remember, we all come from love. This is a simple notion. Many things on your journey are simple but not easy. Just remember, you are from love.

Trust in your heart to know when it is right to tell another that you are gay. Some individuals are not in touch with their light and may judge because of their own fears. As you become brighter, you will also attract those of the same frequency. Please, do not allow the struggles of being gay prevent you from shining through in your truest form. We are all presented to the Earth in various shapes, sizes, colors, and forms, with different likes and dislikes. We are all different in many ways in the physical, and yet, exactly the same in the spiritual; different, yet the same. The light that we possess allows us to see through the physical to the spiritual, if we are open to it. When we are in darkness, we cannot truly see ourselves or any other.

Our gift in the physical is to experience all of our differences and appreciate them in ourselves and others. This is to be cherished. It is suggested that you celebrate your differences in human form and know that there is no other like you on the Earth plane in your exact physical form and know that there never will be again. We are all the rarest of diamonds in our physical presentation. This is the magnificence of the human experience.

I put my pen down; a tear fell from my eye. I had never really thought of myself as a rare diamond or so unique in my physical existence here on this Earth. I thought that if I didn't gather another piece of information from my time here, the message that I had just been given would have been worth the journey. I placed my notebook and the pen underneath my pillow and, after undressing, made my way under the mound of covers and prepared myself for sleep.

I had many lucid and colorful dreams that first night. At one point during the night, I awoke and didn't know where I was. I had been dreaming about myself as a small boy. I was playing with my dog, a black Labrador retriever. He was a gift for my fifth birthday. Just as I awoke, I remember dreaming that my dog had been licking my face and that I was rolling around on the grass in the backyard of my childhood house. I must have been rolling around in the bed as well, because every blanket was now on the cabin floor. I thought of how my dog was such a symbol for me of unconditional love. *Was this a message?* The dream seemed so real—I felt as if I was a young boy again. I don't remember ever feeling so free as I did when I was a small boy, playing with my dog.

I was cold, sitting there in the middle of the night, in an unheated cabin, with no covers on the bed. Awake, I now realized I had to go to the bathroom, but there wasn't one in the small cabin. I jumped off the bed, wrapped myself in covers, and ran outside to go to the bathroom.

There was a small outhouse about thirty feet away from the cabin. I made my way there and back, guided by the light of the moon. I stopped as I arrived back at the door to the cabin and looked up at the stars. It was so beautiful. The night sky was very dark but clear. Millions upon millions of stars seemed to fill the night sky. I felt a connection to the stars, one that I could only equate to feelings I had when I was around Bill or in meditation. I stood there for almost fifteen minutes looking at the vast wonder of the Universe reflected in the sky that night. I took a few deep breaths, inhaling the crisp air and everlasting beauty of the night and then made my way back into the cabin where I jumped back up on the bed and nestled myself in the blankets and pillows for the remainder of the night.

Seventeen
Day One

I arose the next morning at about 5:00 a.m. I felt great. It must have been the fresh mountain air. My lungs felt clear, my mind felt clear, I felt free and alive. I decided to go for a morning hike. I got dressed and ate an orange and then took my notebook from under my pillow. I grabbed a water bottle from my pack and headed out of the cabin toward the lake.

I hiked for about an hour and finally reached Donner Lake. It was secluded and surrounded by trees. The sun was rising in a cloudless, clear blue sky. This was an early sign of a beautiful day to come. The lake was not huge, but it was totally free of human beings except for me. I did see an abundance of wildlife. There were birds chirping. I noticed two black squirrels chasing each other on the ground and then up and down a tree. Then, they jumped back and forth between trees. I had brought some nuts to the cabin with me but had left them in my pack. I told the two squirrels that if I came back to the lake while I was here, I would bring them a treat. I moved over to a man-made bench near the lake and sat on it. There were trout jumping in the lake. I decided to meditate.

I took a few deep breaths and then closed my eyes. At first, I had a few disjointed thoughts but then was in a deep meditation.

I was back in the cave where I had first met My Guide. I moved towards the now so familiar beautiful indigo light. I arrived there to be greeted by My Guide, still transparent and unrecognizable.

My Guide spoke. "Drew, welcome to this journey of self-discovery. Enjoy this process; it will free you from past pain. Seek always inside as to the direction you are to move in during this life. Know that you are guided and protected. Know that all of the resources required to make this journey grand are within you. You are truly blessed in this lifetime. Discover who you are and what it is that you truly believe. It is requested that you write this down as a reminder to your-

self for future reference. Know that the information given to you is your truth."

The faint image then seemed to disappear into the brightness of the indigo light. I couldn't help but wonder why My Guide's image was still so faint and unclear. My face was feeling warm, so I opened my eyes. The sun was now shining directly upon me. I was feeling the need to open my journal and write.

I wrote down a question.

HOW DID THE WORLD BEGIN?

I was amazed that I would ask this monumental question, but then placed my pen to paper and transcribed the answer.

The world was created by the light of God. A scientist would explain it to you as a series of explosions within the Universe. The essence of it is that it was created by God energy—the same energy that you are much a part of.

HOW DO I KNOW THAT I AM A PART OF THIS GOD ENERGY?

Drew, a question to you in return. How could you not be? As if your existence in human form is not proof of this miracle in itself. The intricacies of the development of the human body changing from two cells to four to eight and soon developing into the human form, is unmatched by anything else that is of God. And although science on your plane will be picking and probing the human body forever to discover its mysteries, it is still in its infancy in terms of understanding the heart, the soul, and the mind. The existence of this triad allows you to connect with the Universe, of which you are a part. You are connected to the Universe, and this is proof that you are part of the God energy. Look around at the place you find yourself in at this very moment. Where did it come from? How was this beauty created? Do you feel connected or not?

I stopped writing and looked around at the place I was at that very moment. That place, the lake, the mountains, the flowers, the blue sky, the wildlife; it was all so beautiful. I did feel extremely connected to that place. I felt extremely blessed and at peace and very much a part of my surroundings.

I wrote the next question.

IS GOD AN ALMIGHTY FIGURE?

God is an all-loving energy. Remember, God is much like the gravity which you cannot see, and we are all a part of this energy.

WHAT IS RELIGION?

Religion is a system that was created by human beings. It has become much more of an institution today. Much of religion was created to unite human beings in love.

THEN WHY DO SOME RELIGIONS CONDEMN CERTAIN GROUPS OF PEOPLE?

This is out of fear and disconnection. We are all ultimately connected. There are many religions which have been created throughout your earthly time, and love should be their focus. Love without judgment. But, rules and regulations are of the human creation and not of God. When any human being condemns another, this we equate to a form of judgment.

WHAT ABOUT BEING GAY AND RELIGION?

Please be reminded, religion is man-made; spirituality is God given. We are all spiritual creatures here in the human experience. Spirituality is of God, and the light, and religion is a creation within the human experience. Spirituality is a reflection of the true love of God in its highest form. Spirituality knows no judgment and knows no separation. Being gay has no judgment from the spiritual sense because we are all from the same source, from love. The love of God, and the light, knows nothing of discrimination in any form whatsoever.

THEN WHY DO SO MANY PEOPLE AND RELIGIONS JUDGE HOMOSEXUALITY?

Simply, this is a fear response. Groups of human beings are judged because of their differences. The human condition requires differences or diversities.

We are all different in the human form. Many forget this. It is in the appearance of our outer differences that we are separate. Be reminded that we are all of the spirit and of the light. The Earth plane is moving towards love, and every life form has the free will to express this always. Choose to offer love and not an expression of darkness or fear. Remember, fear is a choice.

HOW DO WE ELIMINATE FEAR?

Continue to offer love at every opportunity and in every interaction with others. Fear can appear to be strong, but remember, you have the choice to choose and offer love. Remember the man you assisted in the parking lot of the health club? Your choice was to offer him love and not fear as an expression of anger or retaliation. Be also reminded that fear is not real.

I stopped for a moment and remembered that day with Mark in the parking lot. I was glad that I had offered to help him. I wrote another question.

FEAR SEEMS VERY REAL TO ME AT TIMES. WHY IS THIS?

Fear arises in the absence of love or light. It is only darkness, nothing more. Remember who you are on the Earth plane. Fear arises out of our forgetfulness of the fact that we are as God and very much a part of the light. We must be conscious to remember who we truly are. We do this by connecting with our source through choosing love and connecting through our loving deeds towards others.

Remember to slow your life at times and connect with your Source. Meditation is a way to do this. Life offers many distractions. One gift you were given for this human experience is the gift of free will. Please use it wisely.

IS THERE SUCH A THING AS A DIVINE PLAN?

Drew, there is a divine plan, and on the Earth plane, it changes daily. Let an explanation follow. Every human spirit has the free will to choose in each and every moment of existence a response. One choice may affect another in succession. It is as if a pebble was cast into a pond, creating many ripples. The divine plan is that of love, joy, freedom, and expansion, and is always to return to love. It is constantly reshaping and unfolding. One may choose love, and another may choose differently. All human beings are offered the opportunity to always choose love and to seek joy, and that is the divine plan for each and every one. The more that choose love, the more love there will be on the Earth plane. It is suggested to you to operate from and offer love in its purest most unconditional form. The lesson is for everyone to choose love in every moment. The Universal divine plan knows only love.

THIS SEEMS IMPOSSIBLE.

It is not easy when the human ego as it is known is attached. This is why we need to be connected to our source constantly. Jesus was an example of this form of love. There are others as well. When the God mind is centered in love, it is not difficult. It is suggested that it start with you. Be the example. An earthly expression follows, "When I change, the world changes."

WHY ARE WE UNABLE TO CHOOSE LOVE IN EVERY SITUATION?

We are all here in different stages of spiritual growth. Some are more in touch with the love or light than others. The gift of our free will offers us the chance to correct what is referred to as a "mistake," and then we may choose love the next time. Human existence is a lifelong school. Growth comes through trying until we get it right.

I was hesitant about writing the next question, but did so anyway.

WHY DO PEOPLE MURDER OTHERS?

One that takes the life in human form of another is living in darkness, disconnected from their source.

WHY DOES THE MURDERER MAKE THIS CHOICE?

Out of fear and the denial of their God self. It is a spiritual process on classroom Earth. All are in different stages on the journey. The love of one may help to heal the next. That is why it is suggested to give love in every situation.

IF WE ARE ALL FROM GOD AND THE LIGHT, THEN WHY DO WE EVEN MAKE THE JOURNEY TO BE ON THIS EARTH TO DISCOVER WHAT WE ALREADY ARE?

It is your soul choice to be in the human experience, Drew. It is also your soul choice to arrive back at your source. This is the simplest of explanations.

Enjoy the benefits of the human form. In no other form may you enjoy senses and feelings such as the touch of another human being or the taste of an orange. When you choose to offer love in the human form, it will only enhance every physical and emotional experience that you have. In spirit form or the light, all that exists is love.

IT SEEMS A BIT UNNECESSARY.

The human mind is linear. Spirit mind is multidimensional. It is suggested that you make the best of your human existence and look at it as a playground where you can experience all of the joys you could ever dream of and appreciate your uniqueness in the physical. It is what you would call a "masquerade ball," so much to experience and appreciate, with the mask, representing the physical; yet remembering that we are all the same behind the mask. And that is love.

DO WE ALSO CHOOSE WHEN TO DIE?

Yes, we do. The soul also chooses to leave or to stay.

WHY WOULD ANYONE CHOOSE TO LEAVE?

The soul may have completed its mission here. Yours is not complete as of yet. The soul may return as well to the Earth plane.

SO, YOU ARE SAYING THAT THERE IS SUCH A THING AS REINCARNATION?

In a sense, yes. Souls are leaving and returning all the time. An explanation is in order. Understand that death is not final. Our spirit, or soul, is the light, and it never dies. A scientific earthly explanation follows. It is as the law of physics. Energy does not disappear; it may only change form. Your soul is energy. There have been experiments made concerning the weighing of individuals just before their physical death and then they are reweighed immediately after their death. A decrease in physical weight has been observed time and time again.

WHY DO THE SOULS CHOOSE TO COME BACK?

Again, this is of their free will. The soul may choose to learn another lesson for spiritual advancement. All of these lessons are to push us closer to being the true expressions of our soul, which is unconditional love. The human interactions that we have on the Earth plane are opportunities to practice this. Our soul may choose to do this until the lesson is learned. If the lesson is not learned as has been shared with you, the soul is then presented with another opportunity to do so.

THIS ALMOST SEEMS TO BE LIKE A CAT CHASING ITS TAIL.

The human mind and the constraint of linear thinking on the Earth plane make this so. The lesson here is, once again, to remember who we are in every single situation. If we remember that we are love in its purest form, then we are able to use our time more beneficially on the Earth plane—loving and laughing and truly appreciating each other. It is a type of cosmic joke that our human incarnation serves only to remind us of who we truly are already. This may create havoc for your human earthly mind, but the God mind knows of what we are speaking. That is why it is necessary to connect with our God mind, the all-knowing, all-loving source, and to do this regularly.

I was beginning to feel overwhelmed, so I stopped writing. A part of me was extremely confused about what was coming out of the pen, and another part of me seemed to understand precisely the messages being given. I thought for a moment about what I was being told about the God mind and the human mind. It was like my human mind would question what was being told to me and my God mind just accepted it as truth. I took a moment and then closed my notebook. I looked again to the beautiful place that I was in. I just knew that there had to be an all-loving source, considering the physical vision being provided for me by this place. Nature was an expression of God.

I arose and decided to make my way back to the cabin for lunch. When I got there, I made myself two cheese and vegetable sandwiches. I also grabbed a fresh apple and made my way outside to eat. I noticed that as I was eating, I, for once, was taking the time to appreciate the food that I put into my body. The flavors of my relatively humble lunch were enhanced by my surroundings. Everything I ate tasted exquisite.

After lunch, I decided to take another short hike. The walk turned into a longer journey than I had planned. I lost my directions and couldn't relocate Bill's cabin. After about three hours and some intense frustration, I stopped and took a few deep breaths, closed my eyes, and asked My Guide to lead me to the cabin. I opened my eyes and then tried to listen within. A small, loving voice inside spoke, *"Turn around. Follow the path behind you."*

I turned and began to move in the opposite direction from where I had been headed, and I arrived at the cabin within fifteen minutes. I was amazed at the power of that tiny inner voice.

Upon arrival back at the cabin, I noticed the sky was beginning to darken. I was grateful to My Guide. I had a bit of uneasiness overcome me when I thought of not being able to speak to anyone for the remainder of my time here. I began to think about Rod and wondered if he was thinking about me. I thought about my job and wondered if they had approached someone else about taking the new position. Feelings of inadequacy then overcame me. I was here in this place, and life continued to go on without me. I didn't know where all of these thoughts and feelings were coming from. It is as if getting lost brought it all up. I pulled out my notebook and decided to ask My Guide about my thoughts and feelings.

WHY AM I FEELING INSECURE ALL OF A SUDDEN?

Drew, your time here is about renewal. Old thought patterns and doubts are surfacing so that they can be replaced with new thought patterns and beliefs. The old no longer serves you. Your journey to and in this place is much as the cocoon you have read about in science. You are being transformed before your very eyes. This will be the cause of some insecurities.

DOES MY LIFE REALLY MATTER HERE?

Yes. Every single life matters, more than you can possibly imagine. The divine plan of love requires that every being of light fulfill his or her role in the Universe. It is also up to that soul to find his or her place in the Universe. It is not a passive existence here.

Drew, you are here to do great things. Your life is of the light, but you first must realize this within yourself. Then you will be able to share it with others. Follow the voice of love within your heart. Once you truly find this, stay connected to that source.

I'M NOT CONNECTED TO MY HEART?

You are connected more to your heart every day. When your life is lived daily, through the heart connection, answers of truth will flow, and you will then be living in God mind and human mind simultaneously. You will know intuitively the responses to your life as situations present themselves.

I FEEL THAT I KNOW THE ANSWERS TO THINGS NOW IN MY LIFE, BUT I OFTEN DOUBT THE ANSWERS. WHY IS THIS?

The response to any situation out of love is always the correct answer. It is a feeling inside. Trust that answer and remove yourself from the chatter coming to you from the outside world. Remember, you are the answer to every question in your life. The occupants of the Earth world often provide their solutions for you. Others may think that they know what is the best path for another. It is best to keep quiet and let the journeyman find his own path.

I BELIEVE WHAT YOU ARE SAYING, BUT I GET CONFUSED WITH SO MUCH INPUT FROM OTHERS. MANY OF THEM OFTEN OFFER THE SAME ADVICE. HOW DO I HANDLE THIS?

To know thyself is to trust thyself. It is often necessary to go deep within in meditation or momentary quiet. Breathing is a good way to commence the connection. When the answer comes, it is soothing to the entire body. It is like the feelings you have had in meditation and around your friend Bill. It just feels right. The feeling is of peace and serenity. The uneasy feeling around others and their wishes for you are just that, uneasy. It doesn't matter how many are saying the same thing. If it does not feel right, it is not right. Trust yourself. If you have instances where you do not know what to do, then the action of waiting is good.

WAITING IS AN ACTION?

Yes. It is suggested that you try and do nothing for an appropriate length of time, should you be confused about a life decision. If you choose to take an action which is out of synchronization with your God mind, know that you may always choose again.

I felt good about the information that I had been given and was now much more calm. I ate a light dinner, and after another short viewing of the stars, made my way into the cabin and retired for the evening.

Eighteen
Day Two

I awoke to my second full day alone in the wilderness. I felt so very peaceful that morning. The previous day's mind chatter was gone. I felt a swirling of peaceful energy radiating through my body. It was as if I had been overcome with the feeling of pure love. Love for myself and everything around me. I decided to dedicate this day to the exploration of love, and, after eating an orange, I pulled out my notebook and began to write My Guide.

HOW DO WE OPERATE OUT OF LOVE IN EVERY MOMENT OF OUR LIVES?

Remember, it first begins inside, with ourselves. This resource we must possess first before we are to share it with others, and we must be conscious of this, as well. The form of love may be a compliment or a selfless act in business or a physical gesture such as a smile. It is best seen among true friends. Let this be a resource place for you. The challenge that we are presented with is to offer the same love to those that we have perceived difficulties with on the Earth plane as we do to those closest to us. These are the moments where we need to stop and ask the question, "How do I approach this situation out of love?" It will take practice, but when we remember the connection that we all share, it will then be much easier. It is suggested that starting your day with meditation will reconnect you with your true source, which will carry you throughout the day.

A bit of advice will follow. It is often a wise tool to place ourselves in another's position and ask of ourselves, "How would I like to be treated in this situation?" The answer should always be, "With love." We may then act in the current situation with love as if we were passing it on to ourselves. In essence, this is what we are truly doing. Whenever we are giving to another, we are actually giving back to ourselves the very thing that we are giving to them. As I give love to you, I am giving love to me. Know this as the truth.

BUT IT SEEMS THAT THE OTHER PERSON MAY NOT BE INTERESTED IN GIVING LOVE BACK TO ME.

This is when we need to give love the most. The other soul, if operating out of darkness, is gasping for love. This is truly what we all seek.

The earthly symbols of money, fame, power, and praise are all substitutions for the unconditional love that we all truly seek. We want the love that we perceive these things will bring to us.

The angry individual needs love the most in those moments of anger. We need to look past the illusion and love without judgment. If we then give love, unconditionally, this then is the most blessed of gifts. No one truly operates out of what you label as hate. We ask that you replace this thinking and know that the other individual is crying for love.

WHAT ABOUT INTIMATE LOVE?

Intimate love is a beautiful experience. There are those spiritual beings in human form with whom we have past connections to, and we often seek out these individuals to reconnect with. Intimate love offers us the opportunity to see ourselves as a reflection. It can be intense from time to time. And this intensity shows us the grand possibilities of our love. We have the opportunity to look inside during these types of interactions as well, to see ourselves as we truly are. Intimate love is wondrous, and when we experience it unconditionally, it only assists in our opening up to love ourselves as well as others.

WHAT ABOUT GAY INTIMATE LOVE?

It is no different. Love is love. Drew, you are trying to separate yourself with these questions. Intimate love between two individuals of a different sex or of the same sex is enhanced by the unconditional love connection. Too much emphasis is placed upon sexual acts here on this Earth. Differences in intimate love from what is called "the majority norm" is of concern to some on the Earth plane. A true intimate unconditional loving connection is so little about the sexual act itself. Remember, we have all had the experience of being male and female. Stripped of our physical bodies, we are the same.

WHY THEN DO PEOPLE STILL CONDEMN HOMOSEXUAL RELATIONSHIPS?

It is changing on Earth. We are all to continue our spiritual education. The lesson is to see others as ourselves, and then we can move on to live in harmony. Darkness causes the separation and allows fear to cloud the God mind. It is suggested that you offer those of judgment, condemnation, and darkness more love.

WHAT ABOUT THE RELIGIOUS INDIVIDUALS WHO SAY, "IT ISN'T YOU THAT WE DO NOT LOVE. IT IS THE SIN."? THE SIN THEY REFER TO IS GAY SEXUALITY.

Be reminded, love is all-encompassing and has no judgment. If I say to you that I love everything about you but your eyes, I am then in judgment. This is not the unconditional love of God. God's love is all-encompassing and all-accepting.

I WOULD THINK THEIR ANSWER TO THAT WOULD BE, "THE SIN OF A MURDERER COULDN'T BE CONDONED."

The direction of your questioning is understood. Remember that the God which we know is of light and unconditional love and knows no judgment. Therefore the love is the same for the murderer, the priest, and the innocent child. One that chooses to murder is using their free will to operate out of darkness.

If a man is intimately loving towards another man, it is entirely different. It is assumed that consent of both parties is involved here on the soul level and on the human level. A blunt answer will follow. Gay love is about the expression of unconditional love between two consenting individuals, and it is just as any other intimate relationship. It is about love.

SO, YOU ARE SAYING THAT GAY LOVE IS NOT A SIN?

Unconditional love knows nothing of judgment. If you are a gay man, then that is who you are. Be that which you are. This is part of your journey here. It is suggested that you discover and be who it is you truly are, in the physical and spiritual alike. Love of any type, operating from a true heart level, is no sin.

I stopped writing. I believe that I was wanting My Guide to offer me something about being gay that I would be able to argue with. It wasn't happening. This new way of thinking was challenging the beliefs that I had been brought up with. It was interesting to be offered information about avoiding judgment. I liked looking at things in this way, but it seemed so hard to operate from this place of love all of the time. It was as if My Guide was truly operating from an entirely different set of rules, and from a much higher level, but at a level I could work at to achieve. I truly believed what I was being told. I moved inside of the cabin and grabbed another orange and an apple.

I took some time to thank nature for the nourishing fruit that I had consumed and then went for another hike. As I hiked that morning, I began to feel angry. I wasn't entirely sure what I was angry at or why the anger had surfaced. My mind was churning with an array of thoughts. *What the hell am I doing here? Is Bill trying to manipulate me? Am I going crazy?* As the thoughts came, I continued to walk. I tried to let the thoughts come in and then let them go. I arrived at a small peak that overlooked a field surrounded by trees.

I looked down at the field. *Had I seen this very field before? Was this the field that I had visited in meditation?* I moved to position myself on a large rock overhang above the field. I closed my eyes and readied myself for a meditation. Before I drifted off, I asked my inner Guide to explain the thoughts that had been churning in my mind.

The familiar and still unrecognizable presence appeared immediately in my meditation. We were in a grouping of tall trees. I felt something unseen take my hand and lead me out into the field. We stopped in the clearing and watched as a figure approached from the other side of the field. The figure looked more and more familiar as it moved closer. I then recognized that it was my father. What was he doing here? He approached and then stopped about five paces away. He said nothing. After a few moments of silence, I asked my father a question.

"What are you doing here?"

"Judgment," was his one-word response.

I was extremely confused, and then I immediately felt angry. I was quiet and then felt My Guide's presence move behind me, as had happened before. I felt two warm and loving hands resting upon my shoulders, although I couldn't see them. A forgotten memory then surfaced.

I remembered a time when I was a small child of about ten. I was running home from grade school extremely fast. I had a piece of paper in my hand. I had written a story for my fourth grade class.

I wrote about a secret world where everyone there was a child and all of the kids had a secret special power. They couldn't tell each other what their power was, but the power could only be used to help people. The kids ended up defeating all of the evil in the world with their helping powers.

I was the only kid in class that received his paper back. Our teacher, Miss Winton, read my paper to the entire class and then addressed the class. "For those of you who think you can write that well, I say, write that well." She made everyone rewrite their papers except me.

I arrived home, and my father was there. I was so happy. I showed him my paper and told him that I wanted to write stories when I got bigger. He took the paper, looked at it for a moment, and then crumpled it and tossed it into the trash can.

"Writing is for sissies!" he said.

I had totally forgotten this childhood occurrence.

I looked at my father standing in the field.

"Why did you say such a thing to me? I was only a small boy."

"Drew, I am sorry. I had projected my own fears upon you. I didn't want you to pursue something in life that you may not have been able to make a living at. Writing is so hard. As a parent, you want the best for your children, and sometimes that includes your image of what they should do and be. I am sorry, son. I release you from my life." And then he turned and began to walk away.

A rush of emotion overcame me. I began to cry. I wanted to chase after him. My Guide's presence prevented me from moving, and then spoke softly, "Let him go."

I turned to face My Guide's unseeable presence as my father disappeared into the trees.

"Why?" I asked.

"You have forgotten your true dream here. You have been holding on to your father's dreams for you for too long." I heard the message in my heart.

I was confused. I had buried that memory so deep that I had totally forgotten it. Then I remembered the day that followed that day my father threw my paper into the trash. It was the first day I had attended football practice. I remembered my father's face and how proud he seemed to be of me. I don't really think I even wanted to be there. I looked to My Guide's presence and again began to cry. I felt My Guide's warmth engulf me.

"Your mission here is to find yourself. This is part of that journey. We need to let the past go in order to live in the present."

"Why can't I see you?" I was frustrated.

"In time," was the only answer.

I then opened my eyes. I really had been crying. I looked down to the field from the rock above, remembering everything that had just happened. I sat there and thought about the memory that had been presented to me. It was as real as the sun that was glistening upon my face. I felt sadness, but I also had questions about what I had just remembered. I took out my notebook and began to write.

WHAT AM I HERE TO DO ON THIS PLANET?

The key is to find an area that you have a passion for. That which you love is the answer. The more time you take to clear your mind and to center yourself in your heart, the closer you will be to finding your answer.

WHY DID I HAVE THAT MEMORY?

Growth comes at times through letting go of those things that no longer serve our highest good.

I was upset with the answer. I asked another.

WHY WON'T YOU TELL ME MY MISSION HERE?

It is suggested that you find your passion, Drew.

I closed the notebook, stood up and screamed, as loud as I could. "FUCK!" It felt great.

I moved from the spot on the rocks and began to run. As I did I began to think about my father. *Didn't he really want what was best for me in my life?* I'm sure he did.

I had more thoughts of football practices and remembered hating it so much of the time. I loved sports, yet I hated football. I enjoyed swimming, I knew that. I continued to run. I came to a small waterfall and stopped. I leaned against a tree.

As I stood there, my mind raced heavily with thoughts. *Maybe I shouldn't take the job promotion. Who the hell am I? I don't know what it is that I want. Why did I have to remember about the paper? I hate my father.* I was tired. I collapsed next to the tree and slept for a short while.

I awoke and decided to make my way to the open field that I had viewed from above. I ate a sandwich that I had prepared earlier in the day as I walked in the direction of the field.

I soon noticed that two black squirrels had been making a parallel journey with me for some time. They were eating the small morsels of bread that had been falling as I ate my lunch. I stopped for a few moments to observe the two squirrels. I wondered, *Were these the two squirrels I had met earlier at the lake?* I did promise to give them some food if I saw them again. It was interesting. They were just playing, running up and down the trees, and eating the crumbs I had dropped, just being squirrels.

This made me think. I had this drive inside of me. I had always felt that I needed to achieve something in my life. I felt uneasy and began to walk again and more briskly this time. I was having another memory.

I remembered how my father was so interested in my brothers and me pursuing sports, especially football. Then I remembered one day he sat all three of us down and told us how lucky we all were for the opportunity to play football. He told us about how he had had to pass up the opportunity to play professional football after a knee injury in college. He told us about the surgery he had on his leg and how he never was the same afterwards. He cried that day.

I had only seen my father cry twice in his life. My father was a very successful businessman. I remembered how we used to visit him at his office. He had old football trophies from his college days and pictures of my brothers and me in our football uniforms in his office. I know that my father loved us all very much. *Had he projected his unfulfilled dreams upon my brothers and me?*

I then thought about my older brothers. They had both played football. Jarred, my middle brother, was still coaching kids. He worked as a credit manager for a large department store chain. Frank, the oldest, was a real estate agent. And then there was me, the youngest. I wondered if my brothers were truly doing what they wanted to be doing with their lives today.

I approached the open field amidst the outcropping of trees. It was as beautiful as I had seen from above and in my meditation. I ran through the last bunch of trees as if I was a child again. I then reached the field, tripped over a clump of dirt, and fell flat on my face, uninjured. I laughed at myself. As Dr. Luke taught me, humor is important. I rolled on the golden ground. The sun was shining down from above. I felt safe in this space. There was a serenity here. My childlike awareness lasted for a few more moments as I rolled through the field. I then came to rest and sat up in the middle of this haven. I opened my notebook and transcribed another question to My Guide.

DOES ANYONE COME FROM TRULY UNCONDITIONALLY LOVING PARENTS?

You are asking if perfection exists on the physical plane. As a participant, you are perfect in your earthly imperfection, as is everyone. We are all moving towards unconditional love in every situation. If you have arrived at this in human form, then there is no need to incarnate again. Drew, remember that as a being of light, your soul has made the choice to be here. There are also choices of the soul that were made before you entered this place. One of those choices was that of picking your parents.

WHY DO WE PICK OUR PARENTS?

Parents are chosen to help us grow in the spiritual via the earthly classroom. There are lessons we are to learn in this classroom. Our soul had a blueprint for growth before we agreed to enter the Earth plane. Then, upon entry, we promptly forget it. This is so that we may encounter the entire experience of our humanness. Once we are here, we begin to seek out those experiences and individuals that were in the blueprint; always with the goal of loving, unconditionally. That is the ultimate lesson. The path to get there may present itself in a variety of ways in the physical. Our parents are a part of this blueprint that our soul created before we arrived. The trials and struggles that we have with a parent are often our ultimate challenge in remembering to love, unconditionally.

WOULD YOU DEFINE UNCONDITIONAL LOVE?

Unconditional love is that from which is our source. At the base of understanding, it is about completely not judging others and situations and about total acceptance of all. As an analogy, think of the love an animal offers so freely.

I NEED MORE OF AN EXPLANATION AS TO WHY WE CHOOSE OUR PARENTS.

The love that we seek here has nothing to do with blame. We often like to blame individuals and circumstances in our lives to free ourselves from taking total responsibility for our physical lives and our journey on this plane. Remember the connection to love that we all share. We are given lessons to free those situations and individuals around us so that we may journey on to connect with complete unconditional love.

Remember the information provided you through the memory of your father and the paper. Human emotion is here to guide you. It is suggested that you feel it, express it, and then move forward. The information has always been there. It was a gift, and now you must free your father of the power that you have given him over your life and move into total responsibility for your own life and your true direction. This challenge of being totally responsible for our own lives is one that many do not want to be reminded of or presented with. Yet we will continue to have the same lessons and many incarnations until we realize that we are all of God. We need to realize that we have all been given the inner power to heal our lives, and this comes about through remembering that we are all a part of the infinite love of God. We are all responsible for the lives that we create here.

WHY DO WE BOTHER WITH THIS?

It is all about spiritual growth. Everyone has free will to ignore the call to love.

PLEASE EXPLAIN MORE ABOUT THE FACT THAT WE ARE ALREADY LIGHT, AND WE COME HERE TO REMIND OURSELVES WHO WE ALREADY ARE.

In the Universe, there is no such thing as time. So this has already happened. It is about completing the circle of love, which in and of itself is already complete. Remember, the space and time continuum of the earthly plane is linear. Life is about completion, and in linear terms, there will eventually be the realization that we never actually left our true source, that of unconditional love. This will come through the expansion of our God minds. We need to realize that we never truly left our source and that all is connected. This is difficult for you to understand, but when humans begin to understand, as a whole, the love will totally encompass more and more on the Earth plane until it is all-encompassing.

I had to stop writing. It was as if I understood and yet as if I did not. I placed the pen and notebook in my pack and then stood up. I took a deep breath, then exhaled. I moved around the perimeter of the field just concentrating on my breathing. I felt so free and alive. After a short while, I moved back to the center of the field where my pack was. I took off my shirt and just lay there looking up at the cloudless sky, absorbing the warmth of the sun. I drifted off.

I had a familiar dream as I lay in the field. I rose above my body and looked down at myself on the grass. I appeared so peaceful. It felt as if I was a kite on a string, flying freely above my physical body.

I moved higher and began to feel a sense of connection to everything around me, all of the trees and the animals and the mountains. I felt a connection to all people. I was a part of the sun. I rose higher and higher. I then felt as if I was a part of the sky and the stars and the moon as well. I was as grand as the entire Universe and very much a part of it all. I rose higher.

I saw galaxies and planets. The higher I rose, the more connected I felt to everything around me, below me, and above me. I looked to my side, and although I could not see it, I sensed My Guide's presence.

"This—what it is that you are feeling now—is your proof that you are connected to the entire Universe. You are as grand as the smallest of animals and as amazing as the most magnificent of stars. You are a part of it all. Know that you are love, as is everything in the entire Universe. You are the light, my friend."

I then began to float down looking all around in amazement. Moments later, I was hovering above my body again. I looked down to see the peace and serenity upon my face as I lay in the field. I felt the connection of unconditional love toward myself.

I opened my eyes; I was back in my body. I sat up and took a deep breath, and I felt a sense of total bliss.

I retrieved my notebook and began to write once again, but this time only for myself. I wrote the following:

I am unconditional love and of God. I am of the light, as is every other. I experience the human condition to grow spiritually and to constantly remember that I am of the light, of love. I am here to be my fullest expression in human form. I must share who I am with others. I can only do this by first loving myself. I am then free to follow my dreams and share that expression through what it is that I am here to do. This is how I am to then offer love, unconditionally, to others.

I stopped. *What was my dream? How was I to express it?* I didn't know. I then arose, put my shirt on, and grabbed my pack. I made my way back to the cabin.

When I got back to the cabin, it was nighttime. I did not realize how far I had hiked that day to that wonderful field. I was exhausted. I ate a small plum and retired to bed.

Nineteen

Day Three

I awoke on the third day with uneasy feelings. I was thinking about the information that I had been given during my time in this place. *What if this information was incorrect?* I got out of the bed and did something that was not a part of my normal daily routine. I knelt at the base of the bed, clasped my hands together, and prayed. I prayed silently, asking to be shown that the information I was being given was true. I then dressed and ate a small breakfast consisting of nuts and fruit. Afterwards, I decided to make my way out into the wilderness once again.

I walked with my pack on my back. It contained my lunch for the day, some water, and my pen and notebook. I thought about how well I was doing without speaking to another human being and was pleased with my performance thus far, except for the occasional mind chatter. I knew from my beginning practice with meditation that those thoughts usually subsided. I remembered that during situations like when I was lost, I could ask My Guide for assistance. I had only experienced positive results with this practice. This led me to return to an inner state of calmness.

I hiked south along an unfamiliar trail. I continued on the path for about an hour. The path was continuously surrounded by large pine trees. The trail then began to ascend. I noticed the sound of water nearby and thought that it must be a small stream. I proceeded in the direction of the sound of flowing water. I hiked for approximately one more hour in and among the trees. I had still not found the water. At this point, I began to get hungry, so I stopped and ate an apple from my pack. I freed myself of the pack and sat on a fallen tree for a moment, then decided to write in my notebook.

WHY DO WE HAVE FEAR?

Drew, fear is only an illusion. When you live out of fear, you are experiencing the opposite of love. It is a choice, remember this.

I immediately stopped writing upon hearing the sound of a tree branch breaking. I was frightened. I jumped to my feet immediately and turned, scanning in all directions, trying to see what had made the noise. My notebook fell to the ground. I saw nothing. I sat back down, picked up my notebook, reading what I had just written and then began to laugh. I put my pen to paper and then began to write once again.

A moment passed, and then I heard a small fierce growl. I jumped up, dropping everything. I turned around and was now standing face-to-face with a large brown bear. I froze. The bear was frozen for a moment, too. We both just stood there. My mind began to spin. *I'm going to die.* I thought about my father and my mother. I thought about Rod. I thought about my brothers. I didn't know what to do. I closed my eyes momentarily and said one silent word.

"Help."

I opened my eyes, and the bear had backed off slightly. A thought then entered my mind.

"Show no fear."

I'm not sure where the voice came from, but I welcomed it. My mind flashed back to the seemingly worthless piece of information that I had read about concerning the brown bear in my preparation for the final exam in my animal behavior class: "If you stand up to the brown bear and show no fear, the bear will retreat."

The voice spoke again. *"Show no fear. Stand tall. Fear will be replaced with love. Send the creature love."*

The bear seemed anything but loving. I continued to stand there, as the bear got a strange look in its eyes. I thought of love. The bear then rustled its paws and moved in a threatening manner towards me. I stood still and closed my eyes.

"I offer you only love," I said silently.

I opened my eyes just as the bear's paws dug into the ground only a foot away from my shoes. Dirt flew up on my shoes, but I did not move. I took a deep breath. A moment passed. I closed my eyes again, and upon reopening them, witnessed the bear turn, retreating away from me and into the woods. I stood there until the bear had passed out of sight. I felt strong.

I had never in my life experienced anything like this. I thought that I had just survived my own potential death. I do not know if it was the God thoughts that had entered my mind or remembering the information that I had read about not running from the brown bear, but, whatever it was, I truly believe something saved my life that day.

I sat down after a few moments and had remembered my morning prayer. I wanted proof about the validity of the information being given to me. I believe my experience with the brown bear was that proof.

I reviewed what I had done in response to the bear. From my past behavior and conditioning as a human being, it would have been logical for me to run from the animal. Instead, I had had an insight about what I needed to do, which strayed from what my logical response would have been ... a response that could have been the cause of my own death. I have no idea why I signed up for that animal behavior class. There were many others I could have taken in its place. Maybe the sole purpose of my taking that class was for my life to be spared in this future moment. *Was taking that class part of my soul's blueprint for my physical life?* It must have been. I began to see how necessary each and every one of the events in my life must have been in order to bring me to this point. Everything in life prepares me for the next step. And, it is all of value, even if it doesn't appear to have value at the time. I closed my eyes and thanked My Guide.

I opened my eyes. *Would I now continue on my hike or not?* I thought briefly about fear. I could let it paralyze me or not. I had the choice. I decided to continue on.

Within one hour, I was standing atop one of the most beautiful rock formations and waterfalls that I had ever witnessed. No bears in sight. I made this my lunch spot. I listened to the soothing sounds of the water as I ate. After I finished, I opened my notebook and asked more questions of My Guide.

HOW DO WE ELIMINATE FEAR?

Fear is present on the Earth plane. Our best solution to the elimination of fear is to offer love. It is suggested that you take notice of the theme of love in these responses that are offered. Through the total expression of love, fear will disappear. Fears are blocks to love. What we make our focus becomes paramount in our lives. What we focus on, we manifest. It is once again suggested to connect through meditation to remember that we are all of the light.

IT IS HARD FOR ME TO BELIEVE THAT WE CAN ELIMINATE FEAR.

First, open your God mind. God knows no such thing as limitation. Only choose love in every situation as you did with the bear. It is something that requires continued practice on the Earth plane. With the practice and continued offering of love, movement will be created in the direction of healing. Fear can be eliminated.

IS THERE A CONNECTION BETWEEN ANIMALS AND HUMANS? I REMEMBER BEING TOLD THAT ANIMALS DO NOT HAVE SOULS.

All living things are connected. Animals are very much connected to humans on the Earth plane and on the spiritual plane as well. The bear knew you were offering love.

MAYBE IT WAS JUST BECAUSE I DIDN'T BACK DOWN?

Maybe.

The answer given to my challenging question amused me. I continued with my questions.

WHAT ABOUT DEATH? DO WE CHOOSE DEATH?

Yes. We choose the transition. However, there is no such thing as death. There is the transformation. And when one is finished with their human form, it is discarded and they are then with the light. It is anything but final.

HOW DO I CHOOSE WHEN I AM TO DIE?

It may have been a soul agreement, or it may be a conscious agreement.

I HAVE A HARD TIME BELIEVING THIS.

Yes, this is known. It is difficult to put into your language. Stay connected to your source. You have a destiny, and it changes daily. Every piece of light in human form is choosing and rechoosing throughout a given day. Lessons are learned and forgotten. The ultimate lesson is always that of offering love in every situation, and this information has been presented many, many times. It is only requested of you to do your best.

I DO NOT UNDERSTAND HOW SOMEONE COULD CHOOSE TO BE KILLED IN AN ACCIDENT OR CHOOSE TO BE MURDERED.

You are not expected to. On the highest of levels there have been contracts made between souls about their transformation. There is no judgment in the spirit world, and thus it is only suggested that these souls have chosen creative ways to make their transformation.

I DO NOT WANT TO BE MURDERED.

It is suggested that you will not be.

I WANT TO LIVE MY LIFE TO THE VERY FULLEST AND DIE NATURALLY WHEN I AM IN MY EIGHTIES.

It is nice to know that you are in touch with what you want for yourself. The Universe blesses you in this decision and supports you in it.

WHAT EXACTLY IS KARMA?

Karma is a Universal law that states, "What you sow, so shall you reap." When one approaches life from darkness, then one will experience darkness. When we approach life from light and love, we will then experience the same.

CAN ONE CHANGE THEIR KARMA?

Karma must always be paid off. Yet, one may choose to operate from the light instead of darkness at any time and in any situation.

SO, IF A MURDERER KILLS SOMEONE, WILL THEY THEN BE KILLED?

Possibly. If not in this lifetime then maybe another. But the karma may be paid off in an infinity of ways. A murderer may spend his/her entire life incarcerated, only to meet another murderer, and in this meeting, they may both turn from darkness to light and assist others. This is but one example. There are countless others. Spiritual laws of the Universe are not like the court systems on the Earth plane.

WHAT ARE THESE SPIRITUAL LAWS?

These laws may be summarized in one law: GIVE ONLY LOVE. In everything you do. Ask to be guided on your journey and in everything you do; ask that you do it for the greatest good of all involved. Operate from a place of unconditional love. If you do this, you will always operate and live within ***all*** *spiritual laws.*

WHAT IF I MAKE A MISTAKE?

Correct it and forgive yourself. This is not always an apology which we speak of here. A change in human behavior and action may be the answer.

WHAT ARE THE OTHER SPIRITUAL LAWS?

It is sensed that you are wanting a list or a set of life rules. The summary of these laws is as you have been told. Only offer unconditional love in every situation. A further explanation will follow.

If you are in touch with your emotional body, then we offer you this advice. Listen to your body. It will tell you and guide you. The Ten Commandments are a gift from the Bible. You may want to review these. Remember that there is only love. The spiritual way of life is simple. The human condition has made it difficult.

I stopped writing. Part of me wanted more explanation and part of me thought how hard it was to believe that the only way I needed to live my life could be summed up in, **"offering only unconditional love in every situation."** It is interesting how often I wanted to perceive life as difficult. I did believe what I had been told. I needed to always remember this one spiritual rule and to practice it daily.

I then began to think about perceptions. We all have different perceptions about things as human beings. I had another question, and so I wrote it down.

ARE WE ALL OPERATING FROM INDIVIDUAL RULES HERE?

This is true. Again, remember the gift in the physical world of free will. The gift is a lesson in itself.

Individuals who have strayed from the light may have their own sets of rules. They are missing the mark and yet have the opportunity to choose again. The choice to operate from love and light is always available, and doing so consistently, is the ultimate goal.

IF WE LEARN TO OPERATE SOLELY FROM LOVE AND LIGHT, OFFERING ONLY UNCONDITIONAL LOVE IN EVERY SITUATION, ARE WE THEN FINISHED HERE?

When this happens, a soul has advanced to the highest level and then one's soul and human form are operating in alignment with each other. When this comes to be, a soul may choose to leave or stay. Then, a soul, at this level, may choose to return to the Earth plane.

WHY WOULD THE SOUL CHOOSE TO RETURN IF IT HAS ACCOMPLISHED THE ULTIMATE GOAL?

To play in the physical. The physical incarnation is one in which we have so many opportunities to play, to explore, and to create without limits. When operating from a place of love and light, life in the human form is such a joy.

Another soul may also choose to return as a teacher.

IS BILL ONE OF THOSE SOULS?

Yes.

HOW DO WE HEAL THE WORLD?

When we choose to live from unconditional love and operate from this place, we not only heal ourselves, we are able to pass that on to others. There is an earthly expression, "When I heal, I heal the world." This is an important one to remember.

I JUST DO NOT BELIEVE THAT I CAN OPERATE FROM THAT PLACE ALL OF THE TIME.

You would be surprised what you are capable of.

HOW DO I KNOW THAT I HAVE LEARNED A LESSON HERE?

If a similar situation in your life continues to present itself to you, then a lesson has not been learned.

WHEN MAKING A DECISION, HOW DO I KNOW IT IS THE RIGHT ONE?

The right decision benefits all involved. The earthly expression of a "win, win" decision is one example.

Once again, all of this was making sense to me. I stopped writing. I thought about my paper and what I had discovered from my research on health clubs. Right in that paper, I had suggested the importance of operating clubs from the "win, win" perspective. I thought about Bill and how he talked about having sent customers to other car dealers, if that meant that they got what they wanted. I knew that using manipulation would not be operating out of unconditional love. I was now beginning to more deeply understand how operating out of the spiritual law of offering only unconditional love could be used to analyze my response in every situation.

I thought about another segment of my research, which I had included in that college paper. I had explored rules and regulations and was given advice from one fitness club owner concerning this.

"It is the spirit of the rule," he said.

I understood this. If we operate out of total rigidity and are never able to bend when it comes to rules and regulations, it would create rigidity and negativity. We had recently adopted this philosophy at our club on my advice, after a woman wanted to transfer her club membership to a friend when she found out that she was moving. Our membership policy specifically states, "No membership transfers." This woman had purchased her membership only one month prior and had paid for an entire year. We transferred the membership. It seemed like the right thing to do. The friend who assumed her membership is now a dedicated and happy member. She has even referred three of her friends to our club, all of whom have joined. I thought this was a perfect example of the "win, win" philosophy. I picked up my pen again and wrote another question.

DO SOME PEOPLE HAVE MORE THAN ONE OCCUPATION THAT BEST SUITS THEM ON EARTH?

Yes. It is suggested that everyone's first occupation be to offer unconditional love. To further answer your question, the following explanation is offered. It is understood that you have created a system concerning monetary exchange for goods and services on the Earth plane and know that most choose employment that produces a financial return. There are places we occupy in life, and then, when it is time, we move on. This applies to the working world as well. Trust inside when it is time for you to move on from a place of employment. You are reminded of your free will to choose the type of work that you do. Remember first, to offer unconditional love. This can be accomplished at any workplace. As one advances on their journey, they may choose to fill an occupation in which they may offer unconditional love to more and more.

I thought My Guide would tell me what I was to do about the promotion offer. It didn't happen.

I looked up to the sky and noticed that the sun was beginning to set. I wondered where the time could have gone. This day had passed so quickly. I gathered my things and made my way back to the cabin.

I was extremely exhausted. I drank some water, and then before I went to bed, I decided to pray again. I knelt at the base of the bed and thanked My Guide for being with me that day. I then climbed into bed and drifted off into a peaceful slumber.

Twenty
Day Four

I awoke late for the first time since I had arrived at Bill's cabin. I was feeling lonely from the minute I arose. I dressed, ate an orange, and then made my way outside. I meditated for a short time in the morning sun. This helped ease my feeling of loneliness. I retrieved my notebook and proceeded to write to My Guide once again.

WHAT IS LONELINESS?

Loneliness is brought on by a feeling of disconnection from our source—our source being God or light. We need to constantly reconnect with God. When we operate first from a connection to this place, we will then avoid the feelings of loneliness. Many try to fill the loneliness with work, food, relationships, sex, addictions, or drugs. It is only when we tap into our source that that we truly overcome this human feeling of loneliness. When we are filled first with the love of our source, then we can be with others and not expect them to be the source of our happiness. An earthly saying is appropriate, "Life is an inside job."

YOU SAY THAT IT IS OUR CHOICE TO BE IN INTIMATE RELATIONSHIPS WITH OTHERS?

Yes. It is not something of chance. We do create the relationships that we experience here. It is suggested that you seek to be whole inside and not look for the other individual to feel any perceived emptiness. The emptiness that you call loneliness. Some advice will follow. If you are in an intimate relationship that is not operating out of unconditional love, you may want to choose again.

CAN FEELINGS OF EMPTINESS COME FROM OTHER PLACES?

Yes, it may be sparked from past perceived hurts experienced on the Earth plane.

HOW DO WE OVERCOME THESE PAST HURTS?

We overcome them by learning the lesson at hand. Feel any human emotion around the hurt. This is a release. Forgive ourselves and others, and then let it go. It is then that we allow the unconditional love in to complete the healing.

HOW DO WE FORGIVE?

We forgive ourselves by remembering to operate out of unconditional love and allowing ourselves to be in the human experience and know we will make what are called, "mistakes." We forgive others by realizing the same in them. We may also forgive ourselves by choosing to respond in an unconditionally loving manner after making a mistake. We may invite those whom we have resentments or ill feelings for because of wrongs we perceive they have done to us, into our meditations along with our Guide, sharing our true earthly feelings with them, offering them a chance to respond, blessing them and ourselves, and then letting them go. This is an approach to healing our souls and one you have previously experienced with your father and past girlfriend.

I completed the writing and then decided that I would stay near the cabin for the day. My legs were extremely tired after the extensive hiking that I had completed the previous three days.

I decided that I would straighten things up around Bill's cabin by replenishing his wood supply and repairing a few things inside the cabin. I thought that it would be an unconditionally loving gesture after all that Bill had done for me.

I always carried a small toolbox in my car, which would be more than sufficient to perform the minor repairs that needed to be done around the cabin.

There were a number of loose nails and bolts inside the cabin. A number of floorboards were missing nails. I replaced them. I enjoyed doing the work. I remembered back to the time I volunteered at the homeless shelter in Denver and something that Mandy had told me. She used to be a big-wheel in the corporate world, and she told me that from time to time, she would ask a few of her old acquaintances to help at the shelter.

One day, one of her former coworkers asked her, "Why do you do that work?"

"Because it needs to be done. And it is the responsibility of all of us to help those in need," was Mandy's response.

"I don't understand how you can waste your time helping the lowlife of the world," was the past coworker's reply.

Mandy told me that she had only laughed and hung up the phone. I remember her looking at me and smiling. "He obviously didn't get it."

I'm not sure why this memory entered my mind. I wondered why someone would give up a great job like Mandy had to help the homeless. I knew the answer from the way that she looked. Something that she was doing at the shelter was filling her soul like nothing she had ever accomplished in her entire life, and once she found it, no amount of money could ever replace the feeling she got when she was being of service to her fellows.

I thought about my life and wondered in which direction it was headed. *Maybe I was to be of service in some other area. I did enjoy the fitness industry, but was I giving all that I was capable of and all that I was meant to?* I knew that the fulfillment I had experienced during my good deeds assignment had been matched by no other in my entire life. I also knew that I had to make a living, and that I required money. I felt slightly confused. I decided to take a break from the repair work that I was doing.

I sat in a chair outside the cabin, one that I had just repaired. I took some time to meditate as I sat in the warmth of the midday sun.

I was back in the field lying there and feeling the warmth of the sun shining down on me from above. I remember feelings of total peace and tranquility.

Words from My Guide entered my thoughts.

"All is in order in your life. Everything is exactly as it should be. Trust in this."

I soaked up the words that were given to me. I opened my eyes and was back in the chair outside of the cabin. I retrieved my notebook and began to write in it.

WOULD YOU PLEASE HELP ME IN MAKING THE RIGHT DECISION CONCERNING MY JOB?

Drew, trust that the right decision will present itself to you when the time is right. Be reminded to practice the action of waiting. Many times it is the most valuable thing one can do.

It was as if this reminder suddenly caused a change in my thinking. I knew now that my time at the cabin was becoming extremely valuable to my life, my entire life.

My mind shifted to thinking about why I was attracted to the sports world. I liked to exercise and to feel healthy. *Then why was I feeling less than satisfied in a field of employment that I so enjoyed?*

I had been very driven in sports growing up. I had put in many extra hours at the pool throughout my high school and college swimming career. It then hit me why I had decided to quit swimming after my junior year in college. I wasn't having any fun. I had been driving myself so hard. I wanted to be the best. I think that I wanted to prove something to my father. I wanted to prove that I could make it in a sport that he was less than enthusiastic about supporting me in. My father didn't attend even one of my swim meets. I started to have shoulder problems, and that angered me. My next thought hit me like a club. I didn't need to prove myself to my father or myself any longer.

What all of this meant, I had no idea. *Was I living out my father's dreams for me?* I didn't think so. *Why did I feel the need to identify with the sports world?*

I took a break from my mind's chatter and continued to work on the few other repair projects that I had started around Bill's cabin. I fixed a number of window screens outside of the cabin that were coming loose, and then swept out the cabin.

I had a peaceful lunch and shared some of my food with an energetic squirrel, then went back inside the cabin and took a nap.

I awoke from my nap and continued to work on the cabin. I climbed up on the roof with my hammer in hand and proceeded to hammer among the loose and weathered nails. I looked up to the sky.

"Thank you," were the two words from my mouth. I don't really know why I said them. I just did.

That evening, I decided to light a fire in the small fire pit outside the cabin. I had not done this since my arrival. I made a mixture of potatoes and carrots and placed them in foil and buried the package in hot coals. I remembered having done this as a small boy. I sat and watched the fire and witnessed the sky's darkness overtaking a wonderful and peaceful day. I retrieved my meal from the fire after a short time and ate the childhood treat, enjoying the simplicity of the meal.

I continued to sit and experience the warmth of the fire as the stars made their debut that night. I then got the urge to write to My Guide, so I picked up my notebook and wrote. I didn't ask a question, and immediately when I placed my pen to the paper, this flowed out:

Drew, you are to make a journey for the next two days entirely away from this cabin. Take food and sleeping gear. Trust that you will be led on this journey.

That was it. I stopped writing and nothing more came forth. This was a bit different from my previous communications. I had not initiated any of the written dialogue this time. It was completely automatic. I found the suggestion of a two-day venture interesting. Maybe this was the reason I had chosen to hang around the cabin that day and work on the many projects I had set out to tackle.

I waited a short time for the fire to die down, and I smothered the remaining flames with dirt. Then, after looking at the beauty of the stars again, I made my way into the cabin to retire for the evening.

Twenty-One
Day Five

I awoke the next morning after a restless night. I began to wonder about this two-day excursion away from the cabin. *Where would I sleep? What if I encountered another bear?* I immediately labeled my fears as such and then remembered the words given to me by My Guide.

"Trust that you will be led on this journey."

I had been guided thus far; to think the guidance would cease was not an option for me. I dressed and then went outside to greet the crystal clear skies of the day.

The weather had been picture book perfect my entire trip. I began to wonder if this was a coincidence. I sat on the wooden chair outside of the cabin and decided to meditate. I focused on my breathing with my eyes closed and then asked a question of My Guide before falling into deep meditation, "Why am I being led into the wilderness?"

I was soon inside of the cave and moving towards the indigo light. My Guide's presence moved towards the light and then greeted me. I felt a sense of love and peace.

"Drew, you are to take this journey out of a place of love. Trust that it is necessary and that you will be guided every step of the way."

"But where am I going?" I asked.

"This is a continuation of your journey to truth. You are being led to your deepest truth. Trust the journey."

"Why can't I see you? Why won't you reveal yourself clearly to me?"

"In time," was the only answer.

I then focused during the remainder of my meditation on the word <u>trust</u>.

I came out of my meditation exactly thirty minutes after I had begun, feeling calm and serene.

I prepared two days-worth of food and water. I

readied my pack and attached my sleeping bag, which I retrieved from the car. I left the cabin and closed the door. I took a few deep breaths and then closed my eyes, asking for guidance as to the direction I was to begin. I opened my eyes and focused on the trail that moved north.

I took the north trail and decided that I would continue on that trail until I felt inclined to move in another direction. I hiked for a short time and then came upon a fork in the trail. I stopped. *Which way was I to go?* I took a deep breath and just focused within for a moment. I felt the desire to move on the trail which forked to the west.

I hiked that west trail for about three hours and then decided to take a short break. I took a seat on a tree stump and was immediately privileged with the company of a small bird. The bird was chirping. I wondered for a few moments if this beautiful product of nature was speaking to me. This creature appeared to be extremely tame and didn't move at all. I was perplexed by this. After a few moments of the bird's continued chirping, I looked up and noticed a nest above. I then looked back at the bird, realizing that this living beauty had fallen from the nest above.

What was I to do? I took off my pack and placed it on the ground. I decided to make an attempt at helping this delicate creature back to his nest. I remember hearing stories of birds falling out of nests and then individuals attempting to return the birds to the nest, only to have the mother bird ignore the baby birds or kill them. I felt in this case that I was to help the bird. I knew for certain that the little creature would meet its death if I were to leave it on the forest ground.

I took a bandana from my pack, gently picked up the tiny bird, and wrapped it carefully in the cloth. I then began to climb the tree with the bird in my shirt pocket. This was no easy ascent. The branches were thin and very close together and became even closer together the higher I climbed. After about fifteen minutes, I stood just below the nest.

I heard an abundance of chirping. I pulled the wrapped creature from my pocket and held it in my hand for a brief moment. "Here you go little fella. You're home." I closed my eyes and then asked the Universe to bless this small creature. I reached up from under the nest and then reaching slightly higher, placed the bird in the nest. I retrieved the empty bandana. As I lowered my hand, I noticed and heard a bird chirping from a nearby tree. I spotted the bird and could only think that this was the baby bird's mother.

I immediately descended the tree. I jumped from the last branch to the ground and then backed away after reclaiming my pack. I watched as the mother immediately flew into the nest. The chirping eased as soon as the mother arrived. I was pleased that I had helped this bird get back home.

I put my pack back on and proceeded on my journey. I hiked along the path for another couple of hours, and I arrived at yet another fork in the path, at which point I opted for a southbound trail.

I ended up at a small hidden lake, surrounded by tall pines. There was an enormous rock with a flat top on the south side of the small body of water. I made my way upon it and decided that this would be my lunch spot.

I ate my lunch and then took my notebook out of my pack, deciding to write to My Guide. I wrote my first question.

WAS I TO HELP THAT SMALL BIRD?

Drew, the choice that you made to help the small bird came out of a place of unconditional love. The human condition operates from free will. If you had made the choice to leave the bird on the tree stump, it would have been another situation of unconditional love.

I DO NOT UNDERSTAND. ISN'T THERE ONLY ONE RIGHT ANSWER IN EACH SITUATION?

Not always. Just keep unconditional love in your heart, and in this, your choices will then lead you. You have been told that there is a divine plan and it changes daily. This is one example of that. Another individual may have chosen to leave the bird. This would have been a decision based on unconditional love, as well.

I STILL DO NOT UNDERSTAND.

Simply put, there are many roads, all leading to the same destination. This is all.

SO, THERE ARE MANY WAYS TO ARRIVE AT THE SAME DESTINATION, AS LONG AS WE APPROACH ALL THAT WE DO IN GETTING THERE FROM A PLACE OF UNCONDITIONAL LOVE?

Yes, this is true. Know that if you take a path in life that leads you astray, you can ask your Guide for assistance. It is suggested that you keep the focus of your journey in mind at all times. Your ultimate goal is to arrive at a place of total unconditional love. A comparison explanation will follow.

As an airplane flies towards its destination, be reminded that it is off course eighty to ninety percent of the time. The pilot is correcting the course of the plane constantly. It does, however, eventually reach its final destination. This is much like our lives. We all eventually arrive at our destination of total unconditional love and light.

This information was challenging my thinking. I began to think about the two-day hike that I had been guided to take. I realized then that it didn't matter where I ended up, because wherever I found myself, would be the place I was supposed to be. I then immediately thought that this excursion was pointless. This was confusing to me. I asked a specific question.

IT DOESN'T MATTER WHERE I END UP ON THIS HIKE. IS THAT CORRECT?

You are to spend two days with nature. That is what has been requested of you. It is suggested that you live in the now and enjoy the moment. Be here on this rock now. Enjoy the sun. The present moment is all that we have. The past is only reflection and the future a dream. Everything that we experience happens in the current moment.

I didn't feel that my question had been answered. I was, however, making an attempt at figuring out the assignment, and thus, was having trouble being in the present moment. Maybe I didn't have to know right now. I then placed my notebook in my pack, and after feeling the rock beneath me in the present moment, lay back. I felt the sun above. I listened to the sounds of this place I was in. I heard the water. I heard birds. I heard a fly. I felt a gentle breeze upon my face.

With my eyes closed, I wondered how much I had missed of my life by not actually living in the present moment. Many times, I was thinking about the future. Many times, I focused on past situations. My Guide had provided enlightening information.

I brought myself back to the present, lying upon the rocks. I concentrated once again on this specific moment. I heard the water bouncing off of the base of the rocks. I then heard a fish jump in the lake. Across the lake, I heard a squirrel leap from one tree to another. I heard a small branch fall from a tree. I felt a newfound peace inside of me at this very moment in my life. *Could my life be like this all of the time, enriched, through all of my senses, by living totally in each and every present moment?* Upon thinking this, I heard a small, still voice from inside speak to me.

"Your serenity is within you. Nothing that happens outside of you can affect the peace within unless you choose to allow it."

I began to wonder if I had allowed things in my life, including people and situations, to affect me? I knew that I had. The small, still voice spoke again.

"You are the master of your life."

At that moment, I was at peace with my life, if only for a single instant. Another message was delivered.

"In doing nothing, we are provided the opportunity to confront who we truly are. The art of doing nothing brings us into being."

I was really beginning to believe these words. I sat up on the rocks and looked at the blue sky. My mind and body felt clear. I took a few moments and then stood. I picked up my pack and decided to make my way around to the west side of the lake.

I arrived at the west side of the lake and noticed that the trail led away from the lake. I briefly thought of where I was to make my camp for that evening. The area I was in was new to me. I then began to feel anxious. *Where was I to camp?*

I moved along the west trail and away from the lake. I encountered many forks in the trail and just went whichever way my feet decided to move in at the time. I didn't put much thought into which direction I was heading. At one point, I began to wonder if I would ever be able to find my way back to the cabin after two days. I brought myself back to the current moment by concentrating on my breathing.

I began to notice everything that was happening around me. A small cluster of clouds passed overhead. A few birds seemed to move throughout the same section of woods that I found myself in. I wondered if they could possibly be guiding me. Maybe I was guiding them. I spoke with the birds as I walked along.

"Hey guys, how's it going today?" I tried to keep the conversation light. "What are you guys up to?" I then became entirely conscious of what it was that I was doing. I was talking to birds! I laughed out loud wondering if I was going crazy. And then a thought occurred: *The importance of humor.* I noticed that after I would ask a question of the birds, they would fly over, perch in a nearby tree, and chirp. I stopped and asked them, "Hey guys, are you talking to me?"

The response was a chirp, and so I guessed the answer to be, "Yes."

"Hey guys, who is guiding who here?"

Three birds flew past and chirped again.

I began to think about this moment. *Maybe neither of us was guiding the other. Maybe our lives were in synchronicity with each other's, and, by living in the moment, our spirits had crossed a path in harmony if only for a short while.* I felt a sense of love for the birds. Our interaction carried on for some time. I had never had an experience like this in my entire lifetime.

I stopped for a break to eat some crackers. I noticed that the birds stopped as well. I broke up a few crackers and threw pieces lightly on the ground. After a few moments, I arose and made my way along the trail once again. I looked back briefly to view my bird friends eating the crackers. I spoke to the birds.

"Take care, guys."

About ten minutes later along my journey, I heard the familiar chirps, louder this time. I looked up to see them flying overhead.

I wondered what they could have been saying. Maybe it was, *"Thank you,"* I thought, and as soon as I did, the birds flew away.

I entertained myself with the idea that they had been hungry and tagged along asking me for food, over and over. When I finally gave in to them, they had flown over to thank me and were back on their journey. I laughed at the thought of this, blessed the birds, and waved good-bye.

About thirty minutes later, I noticed an old structure a short distance away through some trees. I also noticed that the sky had begun to darken. I moved closer to the structure and thought perhaps I had been led to this old cabin. *Was this the place that I was to spend the night?* As I moved closer, I noticed that the place was rather weathered but about three times the size of Bill's. I moved in to survey the structure. I was curious as to how this cabin had come to be. There was no road into the area. It appeared to be very old. I circled the cabin and located the front door.

I opened the door and went inside. The stone floor of the cabin was spotless. The entire cabin was empty except for some lumber and old newspapers placed next to a stone fireplace. I assumed the fireplace was operable. I thought it strange that there was nothing else in the cabin. I knew that this was the place that I was to spend the night. I removed my pack, laid my sleeping bag on the floor, then moved over to the fireplace and decided to make a fire. I had forgotten to bring matches, but I looked up and spotted a box sitting on top of the stone mantel.

I picked up the top newspaper and examined it. It was a business publication that I wasn't familiar with, and it was almost a year old. I noticed that it had a mailing label affixed to it, although it was slightly weathered. I held the paper up to my eyes and read the name on the label, "Will ... William Gustafson." Wow! This paper had been addressed to Bill. I knew that I was in the right place.

I made a small fire, and just as the fire started,

so did the rain outside. I listened to the rain pour down and the crackle of thunder in the distance. This place of refuge could not have been placed in my path at a more perfect moment. I was amazed by the coincidence of all of this. I settled into my sleeping bag, next to the warm fire, and, pulling out my notebook, began to write My Guide.

WHAT IS COINCIDENCE?

There is no such thing as coincidence. For example, when something happens which you refer to as a coincidence, it is a signal from the Universe that you are exactly where you are to be at that moment in time and space. You will notice that the more connected you are to your God self, the more that you will encounter what you call coincidence. The lesson is to be truly who you are and operate out of unconditional love. The "coincidences" will then become commonplace in your life. These are signals that you are living in the light. We ask you to continue your journey and know that as time progresses in your world you will have a feeling of flow in your life.

HOW COME I NEVER NOTICED ANY COINCIDENCES HAPPENING IN MY LIFE BEFORE?

Drew, you, as the many others that occupy the planet in this time and space, have been caught up in desired results and not in the moment. At times, we are so caught up in expecting a desired outcome surrounding a current situation that we are blind to all other possibilities. When we are connected to whom we truly are, we then realize that all things are possible and that answers and solutions may arrive at any time and from anywhere. This is called ***living without expectation.*** *The flow of life is experienced from this place. It is extremely freeing to operate within this arena. Be reminded that when living from this place, one may feel lost, but be assured that if you are connected to your source, you are on the right track.*

WHAT YOU ARE SAYING, THEN, IS THAT THE MOST IMPORTANT THING IN LIFE IS TO STAY CONNECTED TO GOD?

God, Higher Self, Master, Higher Power, Guide, Buddha, Unconditional Love, The Light, Truth, and the like. Whatever you choose to call this source is your choice. And the answer to your question is, "Yes." We need to stay connected to the God self. We need to constantly remind ourselves how wonderful and priceless we are, all of us; same, yet different, different, yet same. We are all a part of God. This is why it is necessary to make the journey into self. When this journey is made deep into the core of our being, we find that we are all of the God energy, or love.

I stopped for a short while and thought about what I had written. Again, I was truly believing what was being said to me at a very deep level. We are all a part of God, unconditional love and light.

I thought back to the message Bill had delivered to my class in college. "Know who you are and share that with others."

We are all part of God. I had thought for such a long time that I was separate, either because I was gay or a jock or Caucasian. I began to cry. It wasn't out of sadness. It came from a place of joy. I was feeling on a very deep level the truth of what I was realizing.

I then wrote the following in my notebook:

THANK YOU FOR SHARING THE TRUTH.

I was surprised that there was a response.

Thank you, Drew. We are all here to help each other. We may do this in many different ways. Finding out who we truly are and knowing that we are all connected is a wonderful gift. Remembering it is another. When we operate with this knowledge from a place of unconditional love, life flows. We then begin to trust inside and act out of unconditional love in every moment and situation presented to us in this lifetime experience.

I placed my notebook under my sleeping bag and then gazed into the flame of the fire. I felt present in the moment and connected to the Universe. I watched as the flame of the fire expanded, snapped, and crackled. I was enjoying the present moment.

A short time later, I decided to eat my dinner, which consisted of a peanut butter sandwich and an apple. I savored every bite. I took almost thirty minutes to eat only two items. I thanked the Universe for the nourishment.

I arose, and then, after placing another log on the fire, moved to the door of the cabin. I opened the door and noticed that the rain had stopped. The sky had cleared and presented itself as a dark backdrop cast with an array of stars. I enjoyed this new evening ritual of viewing the miracle of the night sky in all of its magnificence. I took a deep breath and thanked the Universe for my life. I felt serene and complete in that moment. Another tear of joy fell down my cheek. I took the Universe into my soul for a few moments and then made my way into the warm cabin and retired into the comfort of my sleeping bag for the night.

Twenty-Two
Day Six

I awoke to the chirping of birds and the warmth of a displaced sunbeam shining through the cabin window. I lay awake in my sleeping bag for a short time, breathing in the beginning of the new day. I then sat up and decided to make this the place for my morning meditation. I closed my eyes.

I was almost instantly back in the cave where I had been introduced to My Guide. I was so very familiar with this place by now and felt content there. My Guide greeted me once again at the indigo light. I still could not see him/her but strongly felt a presence.

"Drew, your life can be this way from here on out if you so choose."

I understood this to mean that the feelings of serenity and peace could be a part of my human existence from here on out. I had experienced a deep sense of self-love since beginning this journey. A love that was now engulfing my entire being. I was also beginning to have the same feeling for all living things.

My Guide continued. "It is now up to you as to how you choose to share the love and light that you have found."

I stood there before My Guide without a response.

"Remember, you have a special gift, which is to be shared with others."

"What is this special gift?" I asked. The faint image then immediately faded from my sight. I was angered, "Where are you? Why can't I see you?"

I opened my eyes; I was back in the cabin.

I took a few moments to acclimate myself to the room. I was still frustrated that My Guide was not visible to me. *Why wasn't I told what my gift was?*

I rolled up my sleeping bag and prepared my gear between bites of a breakfast apple, all of the time wondering what my special gift was. I readied my pack, and, after thanking the Universe for the shelter, I blessed the cabin and left.

I trusted that I would be led back to Bill's cabin and assumed that it would take the entire day to return. I had made so many turns that even though I had a general idea where I was to go, I was not completely certain.

I moved back into the forest from the direction I had arrived. I walked along the trail and hiked for about an hour, then stopped suddenly. I found myself in new territory. I felt frustrated. My mind was now beginning to focus on my life back in Boulder. I thought about Rod. I was wanting to see him. I thought about Bill and was excited to tell him about my journey. I also thought about my job. I still wasn't sure what to do about the promotion offer.

I thought once again about my special gift. *What on earth was it? Was it a gift that I could share with others—one that would spread unconditional love?* I brought myself back to the moment and looked around the area that I was in. I had no idea where I was or what direction I was headed. Large trees surrounded me on all sides.

Three hours passed, as I hiked in continued frustration. Finally, I found myself in an area that looked somewhat familiar. I increased my pace and moved quickly towards a nearby structure.

I approached the familiar structure. It was the cabin that I had spent the previous evening in. Over three hours of hiking, and I had come to the very same spot I had started from. I had no idea how I had come full circle. I looked at my watch. It was 1:00 p.m. I was worried.

I moved to a nearby rock and sat down. I took a few breaths, closed my eyes, and asked My Guide for help. Within a few moments, My Guide spoke.

"Drew, you will be lead on your journey. Be not afraid."

I took a few more breaths in an attempt to center myself. I then opened my eyes, and feeling more confident, made my way once again along the trail.

I made an attempt to be totally present in my surroundings. I noticed that my shoulders were sore from carrying my pack. I had been tensed up the previous hours during my excursion and carried all of the tension in my shoulders. The voice from inside spoke.

"Relax."

At that moment, I felt as if the lessons I had learned over the months of working with Bill and My Guide had been in vain. I felt a sense of fear setting in.

I walked on for about an hour. I looked at the sky, which was now being invaded by a number of gray clouds. The entire trip had been one of excellent weather, and now that I was lost, things were beginning to turn ugly. I was getting hungry and had eaten all of my food, having only planned to be gone from Bill's cabin for one night and two days. I had a small amount of water left in one of my water bottles. I then heard the rumble of thunder overhead. I looked up only to be greeted by the beginning of a rainstorm.

I hurried my pace as the intensity of rainfall increased, looking for shelter of any kind. I had left my rain gear in my car, thinking I would not need it. This was not my usual practice. I continued to look up and check for breaks in the clouds, which I did not see.

I hurried along for three more hours in the rain. It was now much colder, and I was beginning to experience the effects of the cold. Then, I noticed a small clearing a short distance ahead of me and made my way quickly towards it. As I arrived, I noticed a small meadow that was unfamiliar to me. I moved out into the meadow and experienced the full intensity of the pounding rainstorm. I looked up at the sky in total frustration.

"Help Me!" I yelled.

There was no answer.

My mind began to chatter. *You fool. How could you believe any of this shit?*

"Help Me!" I yelled again.

Still, no answer.

I was angry and frightened. I thought about incidences I'd heard of where people died alone out in the wilderness. *Was this to be my fate? I had finally discovered many of the truths of my life and what I was beginning to see as my place in the Universe, and now what? Death? Was this what life was all about? Discovering your truth and then dying?* My mind was spinning. I wondered if I was becoming hypothermic.

I moved out further into the meadow against what I thought was my better judgment. The rain pounded on me. I shivered as I walked. I noticed a small piece of wood next to a tree on the far side of the meadow and thought that I would rest there for a moment. When I got across the meadow, I discovered that what I had seen was a 4'x4' piece of paneling that I could use to block out some of the rain. I climbed underneath the wood and sat on the wet ground, shivering. I curled up into the fetal position, to limit my body's heat loss, and I prayed that I should not have to lose my life in this place. I began to cry and softly spoke to My Guide.

"Please don't let me die here, in this place." I sat there for two hours, shivering, cold, and frightened. The entire back side of me was wet with runoff from the rain.

Between shallow breaths and shivers, I suddenly

began to hear a small voice from inside. *"You will be lead."*

My immediate thought was that this was bullshit. The sky was getting even darker; evening had arrived. I then drifted off and began to dream or hallucinate—I wasn't sure which.

I saw myself walking in a field on a warm sunny day. It was the field that I had visited days before—the same one from my meditation. My Guide's presence greeted me there. We approached each other. This moment seemed so real to me.

"Drew, your gift to the world is something that you have possessed your entire life. It is unconditional love. You are a part of God, of love. It is time for you to share that with others."

I thought that maybe I had died. My eyes were open, I think, and at that point, I noticed animals beginning to move into the field. They all approached me. A small doe moved over and licked my hand. Birds flew overhead. I noticed a small rabbit cuddled up next to me. How could this be happening? I felt at peace.

Suddenly, the shelter I had made collapsed, and I opened my eyes. I wasn't dead. I arose, pushing the wood from my back. I moved swiftly back into the forest with a newfound energy. I walked briskly and turned right onto an unknown trail. After a short period of time, I turned left onto another trail.

"You will be lead. You are safe," echoed the voice.

I knew that I was now experiencing hypothermia, but I wasn't sure how long I had before I had to give up, and so I continued on with an unknown reserve of energy.

I think it was about thirty minutes later that I found myself face-to-face with a wall of rock. It was nighttime now.

"Look up," a small voice inside cried out.

I looked up, and there was a small ledge. I thought that maybe there was an overhang above, where I could find shelter from the storm. *But, how was I to climb up there?* There was a tree limb that had been broken off in a small crevasse in the rocks. This would be my only help in scaling the wall of wet rock. I realized I would not be able to climb up the rock with my pack on.

I shed my pack and made three gallant attempts to scale the rock; all three failed. Tears and rain were running down my face. The moon illuminated the wet rock, as the rain continued to fall. I decided to give it one final try. I grabbed the limb, attempting to climb up the rock again. I had almost reached the top, when I slipped and fell onto the muddied ground below.

"NO!" I screamed.

"One more try," a small, quiet voice urged.

I was operating on my last reserve of energy but gave one final attempt. I grabbed the wet limb and pulled myself up. I located a small dry spot in the rock that I had not seen before and placed my hand in it. I pulled myself up and finally reached the overhang. I rested there for a moment.

I looked up and noticed that there was an opening in the rock just past the overhang. The ledge provided safety from the rain, but I thought I might be warmer inside the opening. I moved towards the opening and noticed it was a cave.

I entered the opening, now entirely shielded from the downpour of rain. I stood there and tried to gain my bearings. I was shaking, and my hands were numb. I was dirty; I was soaking wet; I was tired; I was scared. The immediate area that I was in was dry, but it was not very warm. I began to wonder how I would survive the night. I felt extremely weak at that point.

I wasn't sure how big the cave was, so I chose to move further in. It was very dark. I closed my eyes for a moment and asked My Guide, "Please help me."

"Move deeper into the cave," the voice commanded.

I did not feel very trusting of the voice at this point. I took a deep breath, and then, feeling my way slowly along the side of the rock, I moved deeper into the cave. I went about ten paces deeper into the cave and turned back to see the rain, as it continued pouring down near the cave entrance.

I turned around to look deeper into the cave and noticed a faint light. I wondered what this light could be and where it could be coming from. I moved slowly in that direction. The closer I got, the brighter the light became. I noticed that I was also beginning to feel warmer. I thought that maybe I was being led to the other side of the huge rock and back outside.

The light now made it possible to move without my hands guiding my way. I approached the light. It was the most beautiful light I had ever seen, with the exception of the light in my meditation. I then wondered again if I had died. *Was this the place, the same place that I had seen so many times in my meditation?* I arrived at the light. It was indigo, and I had no idea what was the source of this light. It was coming from somewhere, but presented itself, as an illumination above a small formation of rocks.

I looked at the light for a few moments. I continued to feel my body get warmer. The feeling then came back, almost instantly, to my hands. I closed my eyes.

"Thank you." A moment passed.

"Do not be afraid."

I opened my eyes, and as I looked up, standing

in front of me was a presence. I couldn't make out what or who it was. It was transparent. I opened my eyes wider. I wasn't afraid. I looked at my clothing, and it was now dry and clean. I felt completely nourished and without hunger.

"You are in a safe place."

We stood facing each other without words for the longest time. I felt enriched in this being's presence.

"You have questions for me?

"Who are you?" There was no answer. "Why can't I see you?" A burst of emotion filled my being. "What do you want from me?"

No answer.

It was then that I began to cry.

"I am so afraid."

"Be not afraid."

"Why can't I know who you are? Are you My Guide?"

"Close your eyes, Drew."

I waited a few moments and then closed my eyes.

"I am your Guide."

"Then why won't you reveal yourself to me?" I replied, my eyes still closed. A peaceful moment passed.

"It is time."

I was confused.

"Take a deep breath, Drew."

I did and exhaled.

"Now, open your eyes."

I opened my eyes to see the transparent figure now slowly come into focus.

"I am your Guide, Drew."

I stood there, my mouth now wide open as the presence slowly came into full focus. It was human, a male, about my height and build.

"To every question in your life, Drew, you are the answer."

The face looked familiar.

"To every problem, you are the solution."

It was me. It was as if I was looking into a mirror.

"What?" I was confused.

"You are a part of God."

A tear fell from my eye. Then, the most amazing thing happened. The figure began to metamorphose. First, into my mother, then my father, my brothers, Bill, Rod, Dr. Luke, my grandpa, another small child, an Asian woman, an African-American teenager, all within seconds.

"We are all a part of God."

This moment was so beautiful. After a short time,

the image transformed back into a mirror image of me.

We are all a part of God.

I got it. "Why did you let me get lost?"

"You were never lost. It is in the times that we sense the greatest disconnection from our source that we are most connected. Everything that has happened in your life has been cause to bring you to this point."

"But why am I here?" My Guide smiled and looked at me with tranquil, green eyes.

"Your journey into self has brought you here. Your inner spirit has brought you to this place. It is the unconditional love operating in your life. It may be discomforting to your human form at times but the core of who you are must progress on your journey."

"And what is that journey?"

"The journey into light and total unconditional love."

I did believe that all that had happened to me had brought me to this point. I was extremely overwhelmed at meeting My Guide. I never intended to see this cave, the indigo light, this special place, My Guide in the physical, me as a part of God, every living thing as a part of God. The journey that brought me here was one of mystery and one of magnificence. I knew I could never have consciously mapped out the course that had brought me here.

"Know that you have chosen this journey. You are now connected to your true source. Your life will flow as you remain connected."

"What about my job?"

"To life's many questions, you are the answer. God is in partnership with you. To every perceived problem in your life, you are the solution. Know this to be truth. The connection to your true source, unconditional love, will lead you; trust this always."

"Why have I had such a hard time sharing with others about who I am?"

"Drew, this is a result of your fear. You are first and foremost a part of God. A soul choice made before you arrived here was to incarnate this time as a gay man. You are as every other living creature on this planet, love and light. Let go of your self-judgment and the judgment of others. What you experience in the physical is only but a shell. As is the case for every other living thing. We ask you to appreciate the differences, for uniqueness abides in the physical. This is part of the gift of your life, and it comes from your soul—true unconditional love, which, at its source, is God. God knows no judgment and only knows love for everything living in the Universe."

These words put me at ease, and I truly believed them. Another tear fell from my eye. I looked deeply into the eyes of My Guide. A tear fell from his eye too.

"Know that I am with you always. Trust that you are guided in this lifetime. You are here to experience your every love, dream, and desire in the physical and the spiritual. Operate only from a place of unconditional love. If you falter, correct the situation, forgive yourself, choosing unconditional love as your next response. Know that you are loved. You are as grand as the smallest grain of sand and as the greatest of stars. People and situations will be directed to you as you flow through life. See them for the love and light that they are. Stay connected to your source. Be who you are and share that with others. Pursue your dreams. Above all, love."

My Guide then faded into the light.

Twenty-Three
Day Seven

The next thing that I can remember was waking up. It was morning. I was in my sleeping bag, inside of the cave. My pack was next to me. I felt refreshed and at peace as I sat up and looked around the cave. The sun was shining into the east-facing entrance. I looked deeper into the cave to the west and could only see darkness. I grabbed my pack and opened it. It was dry and full of food as well as two plastic bottles of fresh water. I was extremely surprised. I knew I had left my pack and sleeping bag at the base of the rocks below when I had entered the cave. *How did they get up here? And where had the food and water come from? I had only packed enough for one night and two days.*

I pulled an orange from my pack, examined it, and then ate it. I stood up, rolled my sleeping bag up, and readied myself for the journey back to Bill's cabin. I looked again deep into the cave, but did not venture any farther in. I kneeled for a moment and said a short prayer. "Thank you for my life." I then arose, grabbed my pack, and moved to the outside ledge next to the cave's entrance. I looked up at the crystal blue sky.

I threw my pack to the ground below and made the short climb down, using the same limb I had used to maneuver myself up the previous evening. I stood at the bottom of the rock wall and looked up. The ledge appeared to be about fourteen feet above. I couldn't believe that I had been able to scale the smooth rock, in the pouring rain, the previous night. I picked up my pack and put it on.

I hiked for about two hours. As I did, I took in the beauty around me. Then I took a break. I opened my pack and ate a sandwich and an apple. I thanked the Universe for the nourishment. After putting my pack back on, I proceeded to hike once again. I walked for approximately one more hour, thinking a lot about what had happened the previous night. Suddenly, I noticed that I was nearing Bill's cabin. I hurried my pace, and in just minutes, I was there.

I didn't notice the car parked behind mine, and as I swung open the cabin door, I was blessed with a refreshing sight—Bill. I was extremely surprised to see him there. I flung off my pack and went over and gave him a bear hug. I was so happy to see him. I had not spoken to another human being in seven days.

My first words to Bill were, "Thank you."

"How was it?" was Bill's response.

"Wonderful." It was as if I had gone through a major metamorphosis. I sputtered out most of my experiences to Bill and then ended by saying, "I know I'm a lot different now, but I'm not exactly sure how."

"The first time I did this, I thought I was going crazy. But you get through it," he said.

I smiled and knew at that point that Bill had made a similar journey sometime in his past. I went outside and made my way to my car. I opened the trunk and set my pack inside. Then I closed the trunk. I turned and noticed that the trunk to Bill's car had been left open. I moved over to close it for him, and couldn't help but notice the pair of muddied hiking boots setting in his trunk. Just as I was about to close the trunk, Bill appeared. I stood there startled, looked at the boots and then at Bill.

"Have you decided whether or not you are taking the job promotion?" Bill asked.

I looked at the boots again and then back at Bill. Bill closed the trunk.

"I don't think that I am," I said.

"I got a call yesterday from someone who had heard me speak once before, and he has invited me to speak in California."

"That's great."

"They would like me to speak in San Francisco to a gathering of gay businessmen." Bill paused and then continued, "I'd like you to accompany me there."

"Really?"

"I've never talked to this group before, and I could use your support."

"Certainly." I wasn't prepared for what he said next.

"They asked me if I knew anyone who could deliver an opening speech, and I immediately thought of you, Drew."

"Me?"

"Yes. I thought it would be an exciting challenge for you, and that's why I drove up here, to ask you. I need to let them know today."

"The boots in your trunk?" I couldn't help but wonder.

"I got up here earlier and didn't see you and decided to go for a short hike."

I accepted this answer and didn't feel the need to pry any further. I thought to myself that there would have been no way that Bill could have scaled the rock wall and delivered my pack, sleeping bag, and a new food supply to me the previous night.

"So, what do you say, Drew?"

"Sure, I'd love to," even though I didn't know what I would have to say to those men.

"Great. I'm excited to have your support."

We secured the cabin and then decided to meet back in Boulder at the health food store and deli for a sandwich. I gave Bill another hug and thanked him for the use of his cabin. Then we got into our separate vehicles and headed for Boulder.

As I drove back, I thought about how I was going to tell Janet that I didn't want the promotion. I decided that I did want to stay in my current position, at least for the time being, but didn't want the responsibility and increased hours that came with the new position. I thought about Rod and was extremely anxious to see him. I thought about how the time I had spent in the mountains had been the most loving thing that I had done for myself in my entire life, up to that point, and now it was time to move forward with whatever was next on my journey.

Twenty-Four

Bill and I ate our lunch at the deli. I had an enormous sandwich with all the trimmings. All that I had been eating during my stay in the mountains was fruit, nuts, crackers and cheese, or peanut butter sandwiches.

It was nice to be back around people once again. A part of me had missed the interactions. Bill told me that he had really sensed a deep change in me, and with fall just around the corner, the timing was perfect. He told me that I looked so much lighter and that my eyes even looked brighter. He also said that my spirit appeared refreshed. I did feel more alive and energetic. I also felt much more a part of the flow of life and felt a new calm inside, especially with my decision about the promotion. I knew from this point on that my life would be guided. All I needed to do was to be an active participant in that life. I shared much of this with Bill as we ate.

I asked Bill what I was to speak about in California.

"You will have to decide that." He offered some insight, "I know when I gave my first talk that I had gotten the message to 'speak from my heart.' I did just that, and it must have worked, because I have been speaking to that particular group every year since, almost thirty years now. Just be who you are, Drew, and share from your heart. I believe that is the best way to connect with people."

We finished our lunch. Bill and I hugged, and then I made my way home.

I arrived at my apartment building and made my way up the stairs to my apartment. I noticed that an envelope was taped to the outside door and that a vase containing a single red rose sat on the floor. I ripped the envelope from the door and quickly opened it. Inside was a card which read, "Welcome home." It was signed, "Rod." I thought this was a simple and unconditionally loving gesture.

I went inside my apartment and noticed the message light to my answering machine flashing. I had many calls, but only two were of particular interest to me. One call was from Rod, asking if I would like to go out to dinner when I got back. The other was from Janet, asking me to meet her at Boulder's finest restaurant the next morning to discuss my professional future. I was very much of the understanding that she wanted me to accept the offer. I was grounded inside with the decision that I had made and still knew that I would be unable to accept the promotion.

I first returned Janet's call and left a message for her, confirming the next morning's meeting. I then called Rod. I thanked him for the card and the rose. We decided to meet at a restaurant that night at eight o'clock. He said that he had a meeting and that it would be best if I could meet him at the restaurant. I agreed.

That evening, I drove to the restaurant. Genesis was its name, and I had never eaten there before. I parked my car and made my way into the restaurant. I was excited to spend the evening with Rod.

"Are you Drew?" the hostess asked, as I walked in the door.

"Yes, I am."

"Right this way, please."

I was sure that Rod had already been seated and she was leading me to his table, but then we arrived at closed, double doors.

"You may go in," she said, moving slightly away.

I thought this was a little odd and wondered if I was about to enter the kitchen. The hostess only smiled and looked on as I pushed through one of the doors.

Inside the banquet room, I was greeted by Rod, my entire family, Keith, Janet, and a number of others from the health club.

"Surprise!" they all yelled in unison.

"Happy Birthday!" Rod said. I had totally forgotten that it was my birthday.

"It was my idea, but Rod put it all together," Keith said.

I felt so honored. A few tears of joy filled my eyes, and I didn't wipe them away. I looked around the room to see who I had missed, and there stood Bill, Nancy, Mary, Bill's assistant, and Dr. Luke. Dr. Luke was there! I was so happy they were all present. All of the most significant people in my life were here to share my twenty-second birthday with me.

We had a wonderful dinner. I had an opportunity to speak with everyone individually and even felt a new sense of love for my family. I had come to realize during my week alone in the wilderness that everyone does the best they are able to do in their own lives, and that included my mother and father.

Rod stood up and clinked his spoon on his water glass. "May I have everyone's attention, please? Attention." The room quieted, as Rod continued, "I would like to try something here, and I'm willing to start things off. I think that it would be an extremely kind gesture for each of us to share individually with Drew and each other what an honor and a gift it is to have this man in our lives."

I felt slightly embarrassed, and my eyes shifted to Bill. He smiled. Seeing the sparkle in his eyes immediately put me at ease.

Rod then spoke again. "Although I haven't known Drew for a long time, I must say that I am honored to make the journey of getting to know him. I believe that Drew is a gentle and loving soul, a wonderful friend, and a true gift to the Universe and to all of us here on this glorious night." I was extremely touched.

Dr. Luke stood up next to his mother. He had a present in his hand, which he held out to me. "Here."

I moved over and took the cylindrical gift from him and tore open the package. It was a can of something.

"Open it," he said, with a twinkle in his eyes.

I immediately did and jumped back, laughing, as a six-foot play snake leaped out of the can at me.

Dr. Luke reminded me. "Don't ever forget your sense of humor, Drew!"

I moved over and gave him a great big hug.

My mother stood up next, and with tears in her eyes, she looked directly at me. "I want to honor you, Drew. From the day you were born, I considered you a gift. I thank God every day for that gift, and I love you, son." A tear rolled down my cheek. My mother came over to me, and we hugged.

The next to comment was my father. I flashed back to the day I told my father that I was gay. I had really thought that he was going to have a major problem with it; he touched upon this as he spoke. "Drew, son. I am blessed as a father. I have always wanted what was best for my sons. And as the years have passed, I have realized that maybe the best I had in my mind was not really what was best. I have three boys, and I truly believe that I did the very best job that I was capable of in raising them. I may have pushed too hard at times. I may have made you do things that you didn't want to do. But I want you to know, Drew, it came from love, the best I knew how to give. On this special day, son, I ask you to forgive me for the mistakes that I made in my choices raising you, and know that I love you and support you no matter who you are and what direction you choose to move in with your life."

I had never, in my entire life, heard my father

speak so deeply from his heart. I guess that as the years progress, everyone has the opportunity to review their life. I was unable to hold back the tears. My father approached, and we embraced.

"I love you, Dad." At that moment, I forgave him for all the mistakes that I perceived that he had made in raising me. It was as if any resentments that had been present between us vanished. A thought entered my mind. *Was this shift in my father's behavior a result of the healing meditation My Guide had presented me with while I was in Estes Park?*

An answer followed. *"Maybe."*

My father went back to his seat, and I glanced over at Rod. He wiped a tear from his eye. I'm sure he was thinking about the emotional distance that existed between himself and his family. I felt blessed in this moment. The praises went on for about thirty minutes. My oldest brother, Frank, spoke and even brought up how uncomfortable he was with me being gay, but shared that in the short time before I had arrived, he had been able to speak with Rod, who he thought was a nice guy. He even thanked him for a new business contact. He said that he still wasn't totally comfortable with my being gay but knew that I had my own life to live and wished me all of the happiness in the world.

I knew at this point, that if anyone in the room had had any questions about my sexual orientation, they had been put to rest. And, quite frankly, at that very moment, I didn't care. This was a first for me. I thought about how important all of these people in the room were to me and that if I was uncomfortable being myself around them, I would have troubles being comfortable around others.

I was wanting to speak but was not given the opportunity until after Bill spoke. "I offer love and lifelong blessings to my friend of the light." Bill spoke a different language that night, but I understood what he was talking about. I was very touched that he was there. His was also the shortest acknowledgment.

I stood up after Bill spoke, scanned the faces of everyone in the room, and then spoke briefly. "Thank you. Thank you all very much. I love you all and want you to know this has been the most meaningful birthday of my life." I spoke the words from my heart and felt them deep within my being.

We then ate a wonderful cake that the restaurant had prepared. Shortly afterwards, most everyone left. Rod and I were the last two at the restaurant. I had been overwhelmed by this gesture of unconditional love. Rod asked if I wanted to take a short drive, and I agreed.

We drove up to the very same spot where we had gone weeks before—Flagstaff Mountain, with its wonderful view of Boulder below. I told Rod that his gesture of organizing the party would remain a memory forever. Rod said that he wanted to show me somehow that he really cared about me as a person and that arranging the party was one way he could do that. We parked the car and proceeded to take a hike.

Rod and I walked a short distance on an empty trail. As if on cue, we both stopped and looked at each other. I looked deeply into his eyes. It was as though I were looking into another person's soul, and, in that moment, everything around him disappeared, revealing the light of his true being. My heart was beating fast, and I sensed the same thing happening to Rod, even though we shared no words.

Simultaneously, we embraced. It felt so right and natural for me. I considered this to be one of the most loving moments in my life. This was the type of love I had experienced with My Guide and with Bill. But this time, there was the physical attraction, as well. It was a love that was all-accepting and devoid of any form of manipulation. It felt so pure to me, as if time had stopped and that nothing else existed in the Universe except for that very moment.

Then, as if in response to an unspoken cue from the Universe, we kissed. A simple kiss. Nothing was said. What I felt at that moment melded my spiritual world and my physical world into one. It was an experience that I had never had before. I knew that it was right.

Rod and I pulled away from each other and continued to walk for a short distance. We then made our way back to the car. Rod and I didn't speak much during the ride back to the restaurant to pick up my car. We just enjoyed the power of the silent serenity we found in each other's company. I would never forget the magic that existed that enchanted evening.

Twenty-Five

I awoke the next morning and went for a relaxing run. I then made my way to the bench where I practiced my meditation. I took a few deep breaths and moved into meditation.

I was immediately in the cave and greeted by My Guide, a mirror image of myself, now crystal clear and fully visible. I had questions. I asked again about my special gift. I wanted to know specifically what it was.

"You will know the gift in the outer world much as you already know it in the inner."

I didn't think that I knew it in either world.

"Your new journey in the physical blossoms from your connection to unconditional love. Remember, that

to every question in your life, you hold the answer. It is there inside of you, and you must trust in yourself to find it. In time, you will trust yourself more, and this will come from being connected to your source."

I meditated for about thirty minutes, then ran home and got ready for my morning meeting with Janet.

I walked into the restaurant where I was to meet Janet. Fresh flowers adorned each table. I noticed Janet immediately and was intercepted by the host, who ushered me to her table. Janet stood to greet me. She looked slightly nervous, which wasn't characteristic of her. We sat. I noticed a familiar folder lying atop my place setting.

Janet looked at the folder, then lifted her eyes to connect with mine. "Well, open it."

I wanted to respond at that very moment, but Janet interrupted me, "Before you say a thing, look inside." She pointed to the folder.

I picked it up and opened it. The first page was all lined out. The offer had been sweetened. It was now $45,000 for the first year, with a minimum 10-percent salary increase for the next three years. It included medical and dental coverage, a 401(k) program, and generous profit sharing. It was a great offer. Janet smiled, "You can counter if you'd prefer."

The offer could have been $100,000. I just couldn't accept it. My heart was telling me that accepting the promotion just wasn't the choice I was supposed to make.

"This is such a generous offer, Janet. And I am flattered. I will not be able to accept—I would like to stay on staff in my present position, but I just cannot accept this job." I told her how I had been able to take the time over the past week to really get in touch with my life and that this decision felt so very right. It was as if Janet had already known.

She was not upset. She lowered her eyes momentarily and then responded, "I can't be upset. I accept your decision, Drew. And you may stay in your current position for as long as you like. I have never made an offer like this to any employee, ever. I have a feeling that whatever it is you choose to do with your life, you will be a huge success. I had that feeling from the moment I hired you."

Janet's words were like sweet honey coating my inner being, sweet as gold. I admired her as a boss and as a coworker and knew the club would continue to flourish under her guidance. She was one of the few bosses that I ever had who truly listened to and implemented employee suggestions, even giving credit to the source.

We ordered breakfast. Janet asked me about Rod. This surprised me, but I figured everything was out on the table after the previous night. I felt more at ease with her knowing. I told her that I really liked Rod.

"You two make a nice couple," she said.

I chuckled at this. I now saw Janet in another light. She was my boss, but also my friend. I felt a connection to her spirit that day.

Janet paid for breakfast, and as we made our way towards the exit, Janet interjected one final compliment. "Drew, you are the type of person that people just like; you know, the type that you feel better when you're around?"

"Thanks." I felt the same way about her.

It was a day off from the club for me, so Janet and I parted ways after leaving the restaurant. I walked down the sidewalk towards my car to drive home. When I got home, I had the desire to ask a few questions of My Guide.

WHY DID I TURN DOWN THE JOB?

You doubt your own inner wisdom. In time, this will dissipate. Keep the connection to your source. Life will then always flow for you.

I needed reassurance, and with this answer, it came. I had the immediate urge to speak to Bill, so I went to the phone and picked it up. There was no dial tone. I spoke into the phone. "Hello?"

"Drew?" said a voice from the other end.

"Bill?" This was amazing.

"Synchronicity. I don't have much time. I'm leaving town for a few weeks, and I need to tell the people in San Francisco the title of your talk ... for the program."

This made it all very real. I thought for a moment. "Gift of the Soul," I said, having have no idea where this title came from but liking it.

"That sounds great. I'm going to be in Boston, Philadelphia, and then New York, and when I get back, we'll fly to San Francisco for the conference." I was slightly nervous, and even through the phone, I think Bill sensed this. "You'll do just fine, but I would like to ask you to do one final thing."

"Another assignment?"

"Yes. This is the last I will ask of you. I'd like you to make another list."

"Yes?" I responded.

"I'd like you to take a sheet from your notebook and list one hundred of your dreams—things that you want to accomplish in your lifetime. This is only for you. I want you to share it with yourself and your Guide. After you are finished, I want you to fold it up and put it in your wallet—in a place where it will be safe. And then I want you to read over the list every morning before you start your day."

I thought that this was a great assignment and instantly agreed to it.

"Drew, I honor your courage and your spirit. I love you."

This was nice to hear, but it seemed more like a good-bye than a conversation.

"I love you too, Bill."

"Good-bye," Bill said.

I said good-bye, as well, and then hung up the phone. Just moments after I hung up, the phone rang again. It was Rod. I was so glad to hear from him. He asked if I wanted to go for a late afternoon hike and then out to dinner. I told him I'd love to. Rod agreed to pick me up in an hour, and we hung up. I was looking forward to working on my last assignment.

I had many things in my mind that I wanted to accomplish in my lifetime. I had never actually put them down on paper. I took out my notebook, ripped out a piece of paper, and began writing. It took me only an hour to complete the list. I looked over the list and was pleased with what I had written. I would only share what I had written with My Guide. I folded up the list and put it in my wallet.

Rod picked me up, and we drove to Chautauqua Park. We hiked for a short while, and Rod told me that he wanted to show me a special spot in a nearby clearing. We approached the clearing, and I was amazed at what I saw. There was a man in a tuxedo. A white tablecloth had been placed over a picnic table in the middle of the clearing. A harpist sat in a lawn chair near the table and began to play upon seeing Rod and me. I looked at Rod.

"I hope you're hungry," he said.

Rod had arranged the entire setup, and it was quite a surprise. I would have to say that this topped any romantic gesture that anyone had ever made toward me. We made our way to the table. I don't know where the food came from, but we had an elaborate five-course meal. It consisted of an organic salad, soup, homemade bread, homemade pasta and vegetables, and fresh fruit topped with a sorbet. It was unbelievable. As we ate dinner, the harpist continued to play. We laughed and talked to each other from the heart. I shared some of my experiences in the mountains with Rod.

We sat there for almost two hours. We also attracted the attention of a few hikers and even a forest ranger, who Rod later told me was a friend of his. I didn't know who was watching, nor did I care. We finished our dinner, and as night began to fall on the miraculous day, we made the short walk back to Rod's car.

He drove me home, got out of his car, came around to the passenger side, and opened the door for me. He walked me to my apartment, and we stood outside my door, looking at each other.

"Thank you again," I said.

"You are a very sweet man, Drew."

I blushed, and then a neighbor walked by. We hugged right there in front of my door. My neighbor looked back, but said nothing. As Rod and I pulled away from each other, I remembered something that I had forgotten to tell him. "I'm speaking in San Francisco with Bill on October 6th."

"That's great, Drew. I'd love to hear you."

"I'd love for you to be there." There was a short pause.

"Shoot, I'm supposed to be on the road the first week in October, but I'll see what I can do."

I smiled.

"If I don't make it, Drew, you can be assured that I'll be there in spirit."

We said our goodnights, hugged again, and then Rod went out to his car. I stood there on my balcony watching him as he departed, then looked at the night sky. "Thank you."

Rod and I spent a great deal of time together over the next few weeks. He was a guy full of surprises. I loved surprises. I really liked his uniqueness. At times, we would just sit and laugh and talk for hours. I felt a deep connection to this man and hoped that whatever was happening between us continued. We played tennis. We went out to eat, a lot. We went running together. We went to movies. We went swimming. Before I knew it, it was time for Rod to leave town and for me to journey to San Francisco.

Rod left on his business trip on Wednesday, and I was to leave for San Francisco on Friday. It seemed that Rod would not be able to make it to hear my talk in San Francisco, but that was okay. I knew Bill would be there to support me. I continued my morning meditations and began to think about the talk I was going to give.

I asked My Guide about the talk, and the same answer kept coming. *"You will be given the words when the time is right."* I thought this was a bit strange, but it was the same answer I received the entire week before I left.

I was a bit concerned that I had not heard from Bill yet, because we were to leave the next day. That evening, I got a phone call from Mary. She had accompanied Bill's wife, Nancy, to New York. She said

Bill was visiting a friend in New York City that evening—someone he hadn't seen in thirty years, and I shouldn't worry. I should go to San Francisco, and Bill would meet me at the hotel the following day. I thought that this would be fine and thanked her for the message. Mary also told me that she had sent me something that she thought I would appreciate and that it would be arriving at the hotel in San Francisco. I asked her what it was, but she said it was a surprise.

Twenty-Six

I arrived in San Francisco, and having never been there, was taken by its beauty. I got to the hotel and checked into my room and noticed that a basket of fruit had been placed on the coffee table along with a card. I didn't read the card right away.

I settled in and, after looking out my window at the Golden Gate Bridge, I proceeded to open the card. It was from Rod. The card simply read, "Good Luck. Love, Rod." This was the type of thing I enjoyed about getting to know Rod. He did the nicest things and so often, unexpectedly. I decided to meditate for a little while before taking in some of what the city had to offer.

I was immediately in the cave. I asked My Guide what I was to speak about the next day, and the answer was all too familiar. "You will be given the words. Trust that the Universe is unfolding as it should be."

That was it. I opened my eyes, feeling refreshed. I wondered what this last message meant. I thought about it for a short time, but couldn't concentrate because my stomach was growling. I decided I should treat myself to a meal, so I made my way out to the pier. As I walked, I took in the beauty all around me. There were sea gulls, beautiful boats, and that bridge, the Golden Gate Bridge. The sun was beginning to set behind it, and the splendor of the reddish orange structure gleamed forward. I noticed a small uncrowded vegetarian restaurant and decided to eat there.

I had my notebook with me, and after eating an extremely healthy dinner, sat there with my journal open, looking out to the ocean's unparalleled beauty. I wrote in my notebook.

AM I GOING TO MAKE IT THROUGH MY SPEECH?

It will be life-altering for all.

WHAT ABOUT BILL?

Bill has been one of the greatest teachers that you will ever meet in this lifetime. He is such an example of true unconditional love. Be blessed that you have known such a man.

I appreciated the answer. I assumed having had my last lesson that he was now no longer considered my teacher and really felt deeply that my new journey and direction in life was upon me. I closed the notebook and made my way back to the hotel.

I was extremely tired and decided to go to bed. I was looking forward to Bill's arrival the next day.

I had a dream that night that was similar to dreams I'd had a few times before.

I was flying unaided in the sky. I felt so free and loved. It was as if the loving energy in my body was thrusting me through the air. I was laughing and playing among the clouds. It seemed so real. One difference that night was that Bill appeared in my dream. As I flew, he flew up towards me, smiling and looking so at peace. He said nothing, but I felt his presence. He continued past. I then noticed others flying near and looking so peaceful. A small baby passed me. Some others were going much higher than me, and for some reason, I was content to fly closer to the Earth.

I woke up late the next morning. I had slept until almost 9:00 a.m. I arose and decided to take a short run. I stopped at the front desk on my way out and asked if I had any messages. I did not. I thought that it was strange that Bill hadn't called me to let me know his arrival time.

I ran out near the Bay Bridge, Ferry Building, and along the Embarcadero—the beautiful San Francisco Bay stretched out before me. After awhile, I made my way back to the hotel room. I opened the door and noticed that the red message light on the phone was flashing. I knew Bill would call.

I retrieved the message; it was from Mary. She asked that I call as soon as I got in. That was it. I stopped myself from making any judgments and immediately called her back, noticing that the return number she'd left was a New York number. Mary was silent for a short time, then, in a somber voice, she said, "Drew, Bill passed away last night."

I was stunned. My knees felt weak, my mouth went dry, and tears welled in my eyes, as my throat tensed up. I sat down on the bed. "How?"

"Bill had been visiting his very dear friend, who was a doctor. He had asked Bill to speak to a very special group of children at the New York City Children's Hospital. You know, children always held a special spot in Bill's heart. He delivered one of the most amazing speeches ever. It was about life and appreciation for people and living your dreams. I had never heard him deliver with such emotion. There wasn't a dry eye in the place. He received a standing ovation. We were all to have an early breakfast this morning and then Bill was to fly to San Francisco to meet up with you. According to Nancy, he died peacefully in his sleep."

I could only listen.

"Drew, he really loved you," Mary said.

I sobbed, holding back words. Mary told me that she had to go and make a few calls and then catch a plane. She told me that she would call the group in San Francisco and tell them about Bill.

I hung up the phone and found myself on the floor, sobbing like a small child.

I had been given messages about Bill's death from My Guide and my dream, but I hadn't understood. I cried for a long while and then realized I needed to get some fresh air. I made my way past the hotel lobby and was intercepted by a clerk who handed me an envelope. I took it, not looking at the return address, and made my way outside.

I walked a short distance near the edge of the pier, the Golden Gate Bridge in the background, and found a lone park bench and sat down. Tears streamed down my face as I looked out over the bay, remembering many of the things that Bill had taught me. This man had truly been a gift in my life and in so many others as well. I couldn't make sense of his death and wondered if he had achieved every thing that he had set out in his life to do.

A small voice inside spoke. *"The envelope."*

I looked at the envelope and at the return address. It was from Bill's office. I remembered Mary telling me that she had sent me a surprise. I opened it. It contained a memo pad from Bill's desk. Written in his handwriting were two words, "For Drew." The other piece of paper in the envelope was an old, yellowed, weathered, and taped-up piece of paper. It was somewhat difficult to read. On the top of the paper was written, "Dreams for my life-William J. Gustafson." It was a list of one hundred dreams, and next to every dream was a handwritten date.

I scanned the list. 23) Visit Germany—2/13/67. 14) Marry my true love—4/18/42. 12) Sell 1,000 cars—1/08/57. 78) Speak to 500 nonprofit groups—11/08/82. Then, I looked at the last item, 100) Pass on what I have learned in life to another loving soul. This final item was dated the very day we last spoke. I cried. I never got to share my list with Bill. Then I remembered that it was my list, just for me. I knew at that moment that Bill had accomplished everything in his life that he had ever dreamed of. I began to cry again, but this time, it was out of joy. Never in my wildest dreams did I think I would ever meet someone as fascinating as Bill. He was a man who had lived his life to the fullest and had accomplished everything he set out to do. A man who had left the Earth having made it a better place. He truly loved all people unconditionally.

I was so emotional I wondered if I would be able to speak that night. If I couldn't, I knew that I would have to let the group know. I still didn't know what I would say to these men. I looked up and saw a small girl standing with her mother nearby. She was whispering into her mother's ear, and they were looking in my direction. Tears still filled my eyes.

The mother nudged the little girl and she came towards me, holding her hands behind her back. I wiped my eyes and smiled as this tiny cherub approached.

"You look sad, mister," she said.

"I am," I said, continuing to cry.

"Did you lose a friend?"

I nodded my head yes.

Then she pulled out a small red rose from behind her back and handed it to me. "He's here with you now."

"I know. Thank you." I was still crying.

The mother came up and put her arm around the girl's shoulder. "I'm teaching her about unconditional love," she said.

I nodded and smiled through my tears.

Then the two of them slowly walked away. The little girl turned back once and waved. I looked at the rose and knew that no matter how I was feeling, I would have to speak that night.

Twenty-Seven

I decided to take a short walk along the beach to contemplate my talk. I arrived at the beach, took off my shoes, and walked next to one place on this Earth where the land meets the sea. I thought more about Bill and remembered back to the day I had coincidentally encountered him on the beach in San Diego, when he had told me that I was to be his student. He had said, “When the student is ready, the teacher appears.” I now understood so much of what he meant by that statement. I had been ready. My meeting Bill had carried my life to a place that I might never have discovered by myself. I was eternally grateful. I spent about two hours walking and thinking. Every so often as I walked, I looked at the rose that the little girl had given me.

I got back to the hotel about an hour before the evening's ceremonies were to start. The evening was to begin with a dinner. I felt connected to My Guide, but also acknowledged the disconnection that I felt with those in human form that meant so much to me, who were not present. I wanted them to be there with me. My mother and father had declined my invitation to come and hear me speak because of financial constraints. I hadn't asked my brothers. I was hoping that Rod, Bill, Nancy, and Mary would have been there, but life had taken a different turn recently. Although I was saddened, I understood.

I took the hour to ready myself and dress. When I finished, I knelt at the foot of the hotel room bed and prayed. I prayed for the perfect words to be given to me. I then made my way to the hotel lobby where I noticed a limousine driver holding a sign that read: "Mr. Drew Wilson." I hadn't expected this but allowed the driver to show me to the backseat. He drove me to the posh hotel where the event was to take place.

When I arrived at the hotel, I was ushered to an empty table for six, near the podium and the small stage from which I was to deliver my speech. Everyone else was already eating. Soon after I took a seat, someone approached the table from behind. "Sir, your dinner."

"Thank you," I said, looking at the salad that was placed in front of me. I started to eat the salad.

"May I dine with you, sir?"

I looked up and over my shoulder. It was Rod standing there. I was so surprised, I stood up.

"I hope you have room for me and a few of my friends at your table, sir." I looked behind Rod and saw Nancy, Mary, my mother, and my father approaching the table. I began to cry. I hugged each and everyone of them. Mary had arranged for my mother and father to attend. Nancy had set aside her grief over the loss of Bill for this moment, and had come all the way from New York with Mary. They had just arrived an hour ago. I gave Nancy a huge hug.

"I wouldn't have missed this for anything, Drew," she said. "Bill held you in such high regard. His loving spirit and memory will always be deep in your heart." She wiped a tear as it rolled down her cheek.

We ate our dinner, and then it was time. The host of the evening was Stan Thickett, an extremely successful literary agent. He spoke for a few short minutes, gave his condolences to Nancy, and assured her that he knew Bill was there with us that night in spirit. I glanced at Nancy and witnessed a few more tears falling from her eyes.

Stan continued with his opening remarks. "Our speaker tonight is a young man from Boulder, Colorado. Although I have only had the opportunity to speak with him briefly, I have the feeling that he will touch all of us with the gentleness and love that emanates from his very soul. I present to you, Drew Wilson."

I arose to applause from the entire room and made my way up to the small stage and to the podium. I carried my notebook with me.

"Thank you," I said, taking a few moments to scan the room. Then, one by one, I looked at every individual at my table—from Rod to Mary to Nancy to my mother and then to my father. I took a deep breath and began. "I feel extremely honored to be able to speak with you all tonight. I would like to tell you about the story of a young man. His name is Drew Wilson. One day Drew met a man by the name of William J. Gustafson ... "

I proceeded for the next hour to speak of my journey the past months and the life lessons I had learned as the result of meeting this man, William J. Gustafson. I told them how much my life had changed and how happy I was. I concluded with the following,

"You see, I was this frightened kid, one who was so uncomfortable with himself that he wouldn't allow unconditional love in, from himself, much less from others. But I've learned that it doesn't matter if I'm gay or straight or African-American or left-handed; and yet, it does matter. I am a unique expression of love called Drew Wilson, and to avoid sharing all of those special parts of me with myself and with the world, is to shortchange everyone.

"It's like we all have the opportunity to shine in our own light. It is amazing to me that throughout the history of mankind there has never been another individual here exactly like me or like any of us and there never will be again. I think that is so very special. We are all diamonds, and we need to remember that. Everything about us makes us unique in our expression here. Our eye color, body shape, race, likes, dislikes, sexualities, hobbies, personalities. All of these things are gifts to us. It is as if they are gifts from our soul. I want to share one final thought with you all."

I paused and scanned the room. The crowd was silent, hooked on my every word.

"My friend Bill told me that in life we have three responsibilities:

1) To be who we are and to share that with others;

2) To follow our dreams; and

3) To love."

I took a deep breath, looked up to the ceiling of the room. A tear rolled down my cheek. Then, I looked out and connected with every face in the crowd and said, "Thank you."

It was quiet for what seemed like an eternity, and then I heard the thunderous clapping. It went on for a very long time. Then, I noticed that people were standing. One by one, everyone in the entire room stood up and clapped. I was so amazed and didn't really remember much of what I had said. I felt as if I had been given the words that night from the Universe, from My Guide, and from all of the experiences I had been blessed to have with Bill. I picked up my notebook and made my way back to my table, where I was greeted with loving hugs and tears.

We sat and listened to Stan Thickett close the evening. "Wow, I can't even begin to top that. I would like to thank you, Drew," Stan said, locking eyes with mine. Then he made a few more announcements and ended the program.

The next day, we were all at the airport. Me, Mom, Dad, Rod, Mary, and Nancy. We were to fly back to Colorado together. Moments before we were to board the plane, I noticed a man walking frantically towards us. It was Stan Thickett. He approached and asked if he could speak with me for a moment. Stan and I moved aside. "Drew, I have been up all night. The talk you gave last night—your story, the story about your journey, was so amazing. First of all, we would love to have you speak again next year, if you are not booked already?"

"I'd love to," I chuckled.

Stan continued. "Another thing, I don't know if you have a literary agent or not, but if you could put the words that you delivered to us last night down on paper, all about your journey, I think it would be such an inspirational book."

I smiled and reached into my backpack and pulled out my now somewhat weathered notebook. "It's all right here!"

Stan smiled at me and reached into his pocket. He pulled out his card and handed it to me. "I'm sure you'll have many other offers, but please call me if you are interested in having me represent you," he said.

"Cool," was my immediate response.

Stan stared at me in disbelief, yet delighted with my reply. They announced our flight. "Great, great. Well, please call me next week," he said.

I assured him that I would and then boarded the plane with the most important people in my life—the ones that I truly loved, unconditionally.

We took our seats on the plane and prepared ourselves for the journey home. Then I closed my eyes and readied myself for the next part of my spiritual journey on this Earth.

THE END

Rainbow Pride Press, LLC
Mission Statement

The mission of Rainbow Pride Press is to foster positive self-images and positive self-esteem among members of the human race by providing uplifting and inspirational stories and novels in a format that is easy to read and digest. It is our sincere hope that these pieces will make a profound difference in the lives of those who read them.

The founders of Rainbow Pride Press are also committed to build and enhance self-esteem through seminars, personal appearances, and multimedia events.

Rainbow Pride Press is committed to giving back to the community a percentage of profits from the various revenue streams generated by the company and its outreach programs.

It is our intent to be as highly visible as possible and to set examples of high standards, integrity, and ongoing support where we can best be of service to the community at large.

The founders of Rainbow Pride Press are here to do three things:

1) **We are here to be who we are and share that with others;**
2) **To follow our dreams and to inspire and encourage others to truly follow their dreams and aspirations;**
3) **To love and be loved.**

Dale Colclasure

Dale Thomas Colclasure is a two-time, nationally award-winning author, editor, and publisher. Mr. Colclasure was born and raised in the Southwestern part of the United States. He graduated from the University of New Mexico with a degree in business administration and a concentration in computer based management. After graduation, he migrated to the West Coast and began a career in Southern California. While there, he earned a Master's Degree in administration from California State University. He spent a number of years in the computer industry in both technical support as well as software sales. Those years took him up and down the West Coast where he called both Los Angeles and San Francisco home. After enduring grueling pressure in the corporate America "rat race" as well as strenuous travel schedules and sales quotas, Dale decided to make a brave leap into the world of self-employment and entrepreneurial exploration.

For the past fifteen years, Dale has expanded his passion for the healing arts and explored various forms of massage therapy and healing modalities. He has assembled and managed an organization of over 2,500 individuals in the nutritional industry, providing training and support on a multitude of levels. During that time, he has also expanded his expertise in the areas of real estate sales, property investments, and property management. His love of writing and photography has been deeply ingrained in him since early childhood.

Dale makes his home in the beautiful Rocky Mountains where he enjoys the outdoors, hiking, biking, running, skiing, walking his dog, Geno, and spending quality time with his friends and family members. He relishes his newfound freedom of not having to commute to work, answer to a boss, fulfill sales quotas, or jump through corporate hoops any longer. When the fresh snowfall beckons on a weekday morning, Dale is able to partake in the winter wonder along with a few other very fortunate individuals who have managed to find their niche in life, as well!

Mr. Colclasure can be reached at:
Rainbow Pride Press, LLC
6525 Gunpark Drive, Suite #150-117
Boulder, Colorado USA 80301
(303) 267-2155 FAX: (303) 543-0026
Email: EditorRPP@aol.com
Website: www.RainbowPridePress.com

David Jensen

David Jensen is a two-time, nationally award-winning author, editor, and publisher. Mr. Jensen is a native of Colorado. He has enjoyed much personal and professional success in his life. A graduate from the University of Colorado, with a B.A. in communications, David has worked in the entertainment industry as an actor, writer, producer, and director.

David produced, wrote, and directed a series of educational programs for teenagers which focused on *teenage suicide, diversity, alcohol and substance abuse, and death and dying.* These programs have been distributed worldwide.

David is also an athlete and the cofounder of the Boulder Peak Triathlon, one of the largest triathlons in the United States. In 1996 he made the decision to give up sports and race directing in order to pursue his life's goals, dreams, and passions, focusing on writing, publishing, and public speaking.

David has been writing for more than fifteen years. Late in 1999 David decided to cofound a publishing company with the belief that we are all here on this Earth to basically do three things: 1) To be who we are and share that with others, 2) To follow our lifelong goals and dreams, and 3) To love, ourselves and others. Within this, he provides an avenue for himself and other writers the opportunity to uplift and inspire members of the human race.

David is a man with a wonderful sense of humor, a grand heart, high energy, and an inspiration to anyone with goals, dreams, and inspirations.

Mr. Jensen can be reached at:
Rainbow Pride Press, LLC
6525 Gunpark Drive, Suite #150-117
Boulder, Colorado USA 80301
(303) 267-2155 FAX: (303) 543-0026
Email: EditorRPP@aol.com
Website: www.RainbowPridePress.com

Order Form

For additional copies of
Gift of the Soul

Web Orders: www.RainbowPridePress.com

Mail Orders: 6525 Gunpark Drive, Suite #150-117
Boulder, Colorado USA 80301

Fax Orders: 303.543.0026

Please send me "Gift of the Soul: A Spiritual Journey" at $17.95 per copy.*

Number of books ___________

Total at $17.95 (U.S.) per book ___________

CO residents must add appropriate sales tax ___________

Shipping & handling at $3.50 per book** ___________

TOTAL ENCLOSED $___________

Name ___________

Mailing Address ___________

City/State/ZIP Code ___________

Telephone ___________

Email Address ___________

Payment: ❑ Check ❑ VISA ❑ MasterCard

Card Number ___________

Expiration Date _____ / _____

Name on Card ___________

Signature ___________

* Contact Rainbow Pride Press, LLC for orders to be shipped outside of the United States.
** For more than 5 books, please contact Rainbow Pride Press, LLC for shipping costs.

Order Form

Also available from Rainbow Pride Press, LLC

Journeys Across the Rainbow: Inspirational Stories for the Human Race

Journeys Across the Rainbow is a two-time, nationally award winning anthology featuring nearly eighty inspirational stories, with contributions from around the world. **John Bradshaw**, *New York Times* best-selling author, counselor, theologian and public speaker; **Betty Fairchild**, best-selling co-author of "Now That You Know: A Guidebook for Parents of Lesbians and Gays"; **Tim Gill**, founder of Quark, Inc.; **Sgt. Mitchell Grobeson**, the first openly gay police officer in the Los Angeles Police Department and author of the book, "Outside the Badge"; **Dan Jinks**, Producer of the film, *American Beauty;* **W Mitchell**, best-selling author and public speaker; **Dave Pallone**, *New York Times* best-selling author of the book, "Behind the Mask: My Double Life in Baseball"; and **Patricia Nell Warren**, best-selling author of "The Front Runner" and "Harlan's Race"; are only a few of the many contributors to this powerful and inspiring compilation.

Visit us at www.RainbowPridePress.com

Number of books* ____________

Total at $17.95 (U.S.) per book ____________

CO residents must add appropriate sales tax ____________

Shipping & handling at $3.50 per book** ____________

TOTAL ENCLOSED $___________

Name ____

Mailing Address ____

City/State/ZIP Code ____

Telephone ____

Email Address ____

Payment: ☐ Check ☐ VISA ☐ MasterCard

Card Number ____

Expiration Date ________ / ____________________________________

Name on Card ____

Signature ____

* Contact Rainbow Pride Press, LLC for orders to be shipped outside of the United States.

** For more than 5 books, please contact Rainbow Pride Press, LLC for shipping costs.

"Sunrise, Sunset" by Steve Walker

For an extensive gallery of Steve Walker's paintings and reproductions, visit **www.stevewalkerart.com**